PROFESSIONAL ISSUES IN EDUCATION

NUMBER FIVE

CURRICULUM DEVELOPMENT IN SCOTLAND

PROFESSIONAL ISSUES IN EDUCATION

PROFESSIONAL ISSUES IN EDUCATION

GORDON KIRK *editors* ROBERT GLAISTER

CURRICULUM DEVELOPMENT IN SCOTLAND

W. A. GATHERER

SCOTTISH ACADEMIC PRESS
EDINBURGH

1989

Published by
Scottish Academic Press Ltd
33 Montgomery Street, Edinburgh EH7 5JX

© 1989 Scottish Academic Press Ltd.

First published 1989
ISBN 0 7073 0568 3

ISBN 0-7073-0568-3

 Made and printed by Page Bros (Norwich) Ltd.,
Norwich, Norfolk.

CONTENTS

EDITORIAL INTRODUCTION

The title of this new series intends to signal its three main features. Firstly, its general area is education. That term, however, means more than schooling, more than a narrowly instrumental view of a process, and extends beyond the limited notion of an institutional base for activities. Secondly, the topics chosen are matters which excite a good deal of interest and concern, mainly, but not exclusively, because they involve change and development. They are matters on which widely differing views are held: in that sense they are issues. Finally, the series will explore ideas and principles which relate directly to educational practice and to the context in which practices are developed and debated. In that sense the issues raised are professional.

The last few years have seen very significant developments in Scottish education. Much change has taken place so quickly that the process of development has been masked. Equally, practitioners are so busy with the implementation of change in their own practice that they are unaware of developments around the country. If the full benefit from change is to be realised, it is necessary to feed both review and analysis of the process and the product back into the system. This series is an attempt to realise that objective.

The topics will be issues which arise in Scotland, are of critical concern in Scotland, but which will be documented and discussed in a way which makes them equally accessible to an audience furth of Scotland. Indeed, each volume is intended to contribute to the wider educational debate and to inform and enliven the critical discussion of changes in educational practice in Britain and elsewhere. The series should not be seen as a collection of research reports, but rather each volume should draw on research findings and other appropriate resources to offer a readable, lively and rigorous analysis of the issues involved.

The present volume fills a gap in the documentation of education in Scotland. While there are many accounts of curriculum development within particular areas of the curriculum and innumerable reports of local and national working parties on every aspect of the curriculum, there is no single extended analysis in book form of curriculum development in Scotland. Scottish educationalists, teachers in schools, educational policy-makers, and students engaged in teacher education programmes all need an analytical account of curriculum development. This book seeks to provide that analysis.

Dr. Bill Gatherer is uniquely placed to write it. He is an experienced teacher and college lecturer; he has served as an HMI; he was the Chief Adviser with responsibility for curriculum development in Lothian Region; he is an educational consultant; and he has played a key role in the establishment of curriculum development in Scotland. In addition to these credentials, Bill Gatherer combines a deep concern for educational development in Scotland with the capacity for critical scrutiny to which the series is committed.

Gordon Kirk
Robert Glaister

PREFACE

The Scottish education system is one of the oldest in the world, and it is still changing. The curriculum in our schools is the product of generations of thoughtful reflection, experimentation and evaluation. Yet during the last quarter century or so more has been written about it than during all the previous centuries put together: there has been more curriculum development, more debate and more investment than ever before. But the story of curriculum development in Scotland has not until now been attempted. Perhaps we have been too busy doing it to have time to sit back and contemplate it.

In this book I have traced curriculum development through several decades, beginning from the watershed created by the great Advisory Council reports in the 1940s. I have described the administrative machinery set up to develop the curriculum and I have offered analytical accounts of the ideas that lay behind the processes and results. I regret that I have been unable to do proper justice to the many educators in all parts of the system who have laboured so diligently to improve the educational wellbeing of the nation.

I owe a real debt of gratitude to some who have helped me: to David McNicoll for his valuable assistance with passages dealing with the SCCC; to Bob Glaister for his encouragement and support; to Gordon Kirk for much helpful advice and constructive criticisms; above all to my wife Maimie for her expert and unfailing secretarial and editorial services.

CHAPTER 1

THE CONCEPTS OF *CURRICULUM* AND *DEVELOPMENT*

1. *The meanings of 'curriculum'*

Traditionally in Scotland the term *curriculum* was taken to mean a list of courses or subjects required for a given educational qualification. By the 1940s, this meaning was still dominant in the reports published by the Scottish Education Department. In modern educational parlance, *curriculum* can have a variety of meanings. We speak of the school curriculum or a departmental curriculum, or a subject curriculum. In essence, the term now means all the intended learning outcomes of a teaching programme. The school curriculum, then, is defined as 'all the learning which is planned or guided by the school, whether it is carried on in groups or individually, inside or outside the school'.[1]

It is customary nowadays to distinguish between the *formal curriculum*, the *informal curriculum* and the *hidden curriculum*. As spelled out in Scotland, the formal curriculum comprises the subject courses listed and itemised in the school timetable. The informal curriculum consists of activities carried on under the school's auspices but outside the school day. The hidden curriculum is 'in effect the whole ethos established by the atmosphere of the school, the prevailing standards of behaviour, the attitudes adopted by staff towards pupils, and the values implicitly asserted by its mode of operation'.[2]

A hidden curriculum, by definition, is not consciously intended by the staff of a school. For example, the school's policies and practices in relation to discipline form part of the school's hidden curriculum. The hidden curriculum may, in fact, include influences that are contrary to the school's intentions: for example, an excessively strict disciplinary regime may foster rebelliousness instead of obedience. The hidden curriculum is an important part of the school's impact on its pupils, but it is not amenable to general description. It is gradually being recognised, however, that this so-called 'hidden curriculum' needs to be an active concern of the school. As John MacBeath puts it

'While schools have been trying more systematically in the last decade or so to "teach" personal and social education explicitly they tend to have done so without coming adequately to terms with the implicit, or "hidden", curriculum of personal and social learning that is woven into the fabric of day-to-day school life.'[3]

Both the formal and the informal curriculum contribute elements of the personal and social learning which pupils derive from the 'hidden' curriculum. Schools need to be consciously aware of these influences so that the curriculum, as a whole, has desired effects on the bringing-up of their pupils. In other words, teachers should be aware of the 'transactional curriculum'—that is, the curriculum actually experienced by pupils as opposed to 'the formal written intentions laid down by the school'.[4] Thus another distinction is that between the 'written' curriculum and the 'actual' curriculum delivered in and by the school.

The *informal curriculum* of a school comprises all those experiences planned by the school which lie outside the formal curriculum. Although it existed in almost all schools, the informal curriculum was seldom described or deliberately planned in the past: even today, there are few schools where much thought is devoted to planning and coordinating the informal activities which are so important in the school's general educational programme. Nowadays games and sports are integral features of the timetable, but until comparatively recent times such activities as football and cricket for boys, and hockey for girls, were undertaken as 'extra-curricular' items. Most headteachers would recognise the educational value of these activities and expect teachers to give their services as coaches and supervisors, but they would assign them as 'extras', as they would school concerts, educational visits and clubs devoted to chess, scripture study and so on. Thus the traditional Scottish curriculum was always more than a mere list of classroom subjects. But there was a clear distinction between what was taught in classrooms and what was done outside school hours for the personal and cultural benefit of pupils. The educational importance of these 'informal' activities has been well recognised by progressive educators. 'It was when the traditional curriculum was over that the school woke up,' wrote R. F. Mackenzie in his account of Summerhill Academy.[5] Today, in many schools, less 'formal' activities such as drama, sports or outdoor education may appear on the timetable, but their manifestation in the form of school concerts, matches or excursions to the mountains would still be regarded as 'extra-curricular'. Efforts to integrate 'formal' and 'informal' education are now common in primary schools, but Scottish secondary schools are still far from the ideal envisaged by pioneers like Mackenzie.

Two further kinds of 'curriculum' are now widely mentioned: a *core curriculum* and a *national curriculum*. A core curriculum is the subjects, courses or experiences deemed to be desirable for all the pupils at a given stage. Politically the core curriculum can be described crudely in terms of compulsory subjects, but it is more useful to conceive a core curriculum as being the arrangement of subject matter around recognised social trends and beliefs, producing the knowledge and skills which the 'authorities' have specified as being required by all.[6] A *'national curriculum framework'* is a description of the principles, disciplines and expected outcomes of school curricula as required by government.[7] As we shall see, curricula are developed by various means. National curricula—and national curriculum frameworks—are developed by governmental decree or persuasion.

2.   *Curriculum philosophy*

The philosophical and sociological provenance of Scottish schools' curricula remains to be researched. Nonetheless the work of English, American and Scottish scholars in this field is beginning to influence our perceptions and judgements, and it is now possible to understand the curriculum as a plan for teaching and learning which expresses in pedagogic form a statement of educational aims and objectives. This definition of curriculum allows us to describe curricula in many forms besides the traditional one of 'school programme', that is all the learning activities prescribed for the whole school. Thus we can have a curriculum for mathematics or history or 'health studies', but also an 'activity curriculum' which sets out things to be performed rather than a list of subjects. And it is necessary to explain the 'thinking' behind the curriculum design: the broad general ideas about life and society that give rise to the proposals enshrined in the documents which prescribe the curriculum to be adapted by the schools.

The framers of our curricula have tended to propose the fundamental aims of education as they saw them at the time, and go on to prescribe courses of study which in their view are best calculated to fulfil these aims. Historically, Scottish educational planners have perceived schools as agents of social change. The Scots reformers who founded our school system in the 16th and

17th centuries saw education as the principal means of erecting Christ's kingdom on earth. In more recent times education has repeatedly been assigned a major role in the inculcation and preservation of the 'democratic virtues' of tolerance, industriousness and good citizenship. At the same time, there has long been a recognition that schools have only a limited role to play in the transmission of society's values, and in consequence the Scottish conception of curriculum has been largely pragmatic. Society (in the form of the authors of official statements) has asked mainly that schools should transmit the knowledge and skills deemed to be desirable by the authorities and approved by parents and teachers.

During the last hundred years or so there has been a series of conscious efforts to spell out the aims and objectives of Scottish education, and to express these in the form of curricular frameworks. The councils and committees set up for this purpose have identified elements of our culture to be catered for and have set out to identify the forms of knowledge, skills and dispositions to be developed by the schools. Thus they have sought both to preserve what they deemed worthy of preserving in our way of life and to interpret the requirements of our society in terms of educational objectives and practices. Some references to a few of the major reports published during the twentieth century will demonstrate that there has been a steadily continuing consensus.

In 1917, for example, a Scottish Education Reform Committee, consisting of representatives of the Educational Institute of Scotland and the other teachers' unions, the Secondary Education Association and the Class Teachers' Federation, published its report, *Reform in Scottish Education*.[8] The picture of the school curricula drawn here, we can assume, represented the perceptions of the majority of Scotland's educational leaders. Certainly most of their recommendations for curricular reform were reiterated in the 1920s and 1930s and repeated, with some modifications, in the great Advisory Council Reports of 1946 and 1947. The 1917 Report suggests that there are two opposing tendencies in modern educational thought: seeing the individual as the chief consideration on the one hand, and on the other seeing society as the centre, the need to 'equip' the pupil for 'social service as workman and citizen'. When either view is over-emphasized, they say, 'the result is unsatisfactory'. The Advisory Council of the 1940s took a similar view, asserting 'the primacy of the individual' ('the chief end of education is to foster the full and harmonious development of the individual') but at the same time acknowledging that the school is 'an agent of social change' and that the state will 'naturally' wish to 'direct the forces of change' by means of 'some determination of the content and methods' of education. The twin objectives which derive from this dual aim are, firstly, to inculcate the democratic virtues and, secondly, to ensure that pupils learn basic skills and 'cultivate the special aptitudes which will ensure the maximum productivity of the country'. The 'democratic virtues' spelled out are tolerance, respect for reason and persuasion, hatred of cruelty and oppression, willingness to surrender sectional privileges in the general interest, to sacrifice personal leisure in the common service, and 'an international temper of sympathy and understanding'.[9]

The Memorandum, *Primary Education in Scotland*, issued by the SED in 1965, began its educational rationale with a didactic account of child development derived from Piagetian psychology. This was a new approach to curriculum framing in Scotland, and its central ideas—that the primary school is a stage of development in its own right, not merely a preparation for the secondary school, and that every child naturally passes through sequences of growth and development and should therefore be taught appropriately as an individual—still underlies primary education in Scotland. This Memorandum, written by a committee heavily dominated by members of H.M. Inspectorate (HMI), takes it for granted that children will imbibe 'the values held in esteem by society' but makes little mention of what these values are. But it repeats the well established dual aim of education in Scotland: 'The task of education is two-fold: it must satisfy both the needs of the individual and the requirements of society.' Society's main requirement, it says, is for citizens who are 'skilful, knowledgeable, adaptable, capable of cooperation, and as far as possible of leadership'. The child must be made 'useful to society and adaptable to the kind of environment in which he will live as an adult'. The primary school must 'develop in their pupils the attitudes which will enable them to cope with changing conditions'. Children should be helped to become 'happy and well-adjusted' but should be developing 'intellectual curiosity', and have 'the urge to ask questions' and 'the will and ability to find the answers'. In other words, primary education should aim at developing autonomy in the child's personality and intellect. There is no suggestion here (as had featured prominently in earlier statements) that children should imbibe social and political attitudes tending to develop patriotism or any particular set of political ideas. The committee's preoccupation with the methods of teaching rather than with the content of the curriculum led them to produce an educational document that still, nearly thirty years later, echoes the deep-seated liberalism that characterises Scottish primary schools.[10]

The committee which produced *The Structure of the Curriculum* in 1977 included only one government Inspector, though its secretariat was official. Nonetheless the educational aims on which they founded the curriculum they framed were similar to those made explicit by earlier official statements. They take it for granted that 'schools exist in and for a given society' and must equip young people with the skills, knowledge, social and moral attitudes which 'will fit them for full membership of the adult community'. They are wholly persuaded that the 'effectiveness' of the curriculum is to be judged by its success in preparing pupils for the roles they will have to assume in adult life. What these roles are they do not make clear; but they are clear in requiring that schools should help pupils to cope with 'the world of work' and to develop their 'capacity for making informed judgements on contemporary issues', and 'to establish their commitment to those values that are fundamental to the democratic way of life'. And they repeat the basic generalisation which underlies Scottish educational policy, that schools 'fulfil a dual function, on behalf of society on the one hand, and of individual pupils on the other'.[11]

3. The practical curriculum

A broad statement of aims can be made to suit many different actual situations or processes, and to state what is 'expected' of an education system will give little guidance to teachers in schools faced with the task of drawing up lists of learning activities and outcomes. What actually happens in a classroom is the product of many forces: the given syllabus, the textbooks, worksheets and other materials, the teacher's judgements of the pupils' needs and capacities, the resources at their command, and so on. Few teachers are required to make their pedagogical objectives and practices explicit after they have left the teacher training institution. Yet the 'curriculum' being delivered in a classroom at any moment is amenable to accurate description, and in modern education it is widely agreed that it should be known to and understood by the teachers, the pupils, the parents and the 'authorities' responsible—the school management, the education officers in charge, the elected members of the Authority, the school inspectors. For this reason it is now expected that the school curriculum will be described in detail and that the description, in the form of documents such as school brochures or specially written reports, will be made available to anyone concerned. The process of drawing up such documents is not simple, and most teachers still require guidance from curriculum experts who have devoted time and effort to studying the subject. Curriculum design and management is now a recognised area of technical knowledge which forms the substance of training courses, manuals and treatises in all the developed education systems in the world.

Until comparatively recently a headteacher asked to describe the school curriculum would merely have pointed to the timetable. A list of subjects and activities is still the most common manifestation of curriculum in Scotland. But the timetable is now perceived as only one facet of the curriculum. A headteacher's account will now begin with a statement of the general aims of the school, educational and social, and this will often include references to documents which express 'official' educational policies. Any school's aims and objectives constitute a selection from a much greater body of aims and objectives, and it is an important task for the school staff to make that selection. For it is from their selection of aims and objectives that they will draw the content which constitutes the main body of the curriculum. In Scotland this content is, almost wholly, 'given' to schools by the 'authorities'. But the school still modifies the curriculum content in some important ways.

In the first place, it is the school staff themselves who determine the priority given to any subject or activity, and the assigned priority determines the amount of time devoted to it. A primary school which gives high priority to teaching the 'basic skills', for example, will devote more time to language and mathematical activities; a school where the 'arts' are given high priority will timetable more classes in music, art and, say, drama; a school giving 'outdoor education' priority will devote time to out-of-school activities which other schools will simply not include in the curriculum. Thus the actual curriculum cannot be perceived merely as a list of things taught.

Secondly, it is the teachers who select the methods of teaching any particular subject or skill. Among all the schools which purport to teach language skills, for example, there will be great differences in approach and consequently in the actual classroom activities which constitute language teaching. At one end of the range teachers may proceed formally through expository lessons, textbooks, exercises and tests; at the other end teachers may conduct most or all of their teaching through projects, assigned tasks, theme studies and other 'progressive' techniques. It cannot be said that schools with such radically different methods are delivering the same curriculum.

It is the teachers, essentially, who determine the 'balance' of the curriculum—the combination of selected activities, priorities and approaches which give the curriculum its character and effect. As we shall see, it is in achieving a particular balance that curriculum development finds its main purposes in primary education. The curriculum balance arises from the school's selection of content, the staff's selection of teaching approaches, the way they design the activities from which pupils learn, and the methods by which they provide themselves with the means of estimating pupils' progress. In the Scottish primary schools this balance was not, until recently, a perceived reality: it arose accidentally, because individual teachers were largely left to determine for themselves how they taught the subjects prescribed, within limits that used to be set by examinations. In the secondary schools, the balance of the curriculum is still to some extent accidental, but we are now more conscious of the need to design a 'total learning environment' in which different contributory disciplines are coordinated.

4. The curriculum development process

Curriculum development can be seen to operate at different levels of generality. At the upper, most general (least specific) level we have the content of reports, books, articles, lectures and scholarly studies. At the next-down level we have the more specific works produced by curriculum planners and innovators of various sorts: reports issued by consultative committees, working parties, inspectorate panels, examination boards, research teams and so on. These are applicative works, proposing actual approaches, describing the content and methodology of syllabuses etc., providing model teaching programmes for specified teacher groups. In Scotland, as we shall see, these works have mostly emerged from governmental agencies; but they have occasionally emanated from autonomous agencies such as teams of college staff or regional working parties. At this level, however, we must take account of the powerful role played by textbook writers and publishers.

At the next-down level of development the local education authority operates. The Education Authority (EA) is legally responsible for the curricula in its schools, and in Scotland, as we shall see, there has in recent years been a great amount of practical curriculum development at local level. The modern curriculum is partly shaped by the work of local education officers, advisers and teacher groups.

At the level of greatest specificity (and least generality) lies the school itself. Although it is customary to depict curriculum development as operating in a downward movement, from the 'top' national level to the 'bottom' school level, it is the school itself which is the most important development agency. This is not only because the teacher is the ultimate arbiter of what he or she actually conveys in the classroom—in a real sense the individual pupil determines what is actually learned—

but also because it is the teachers who do the all-important final selection of content, methods and values which constitute the curriculum. Because of this truth, curriculum cannot be defined simplistically as a set of instructions or guidelines handed down to the teachers: it must be perceived as a dynamic process, always changing in accordance with the professional judgements of individual teachers. This has not been understood in Scotland until recently; and for that reason the importance of curriculum development at school level has been seriously underestimated.

Figure 1 shows the relationship of different contributors to the curriculum development process in Scotland.

5. The meanings of 'development'

It will be seen that, at different levels and in the perceptions of different agencies, the term 'development' takes on a variety of meanings. At the highest level of generality it is a process of explication, definition and prescription. At the national, professional level, it is the production and dissemination of materials designed to effect change in the practices of teachers. At the local level it is the production of materials designed to help teachers effect the required changes in their classroom work. At school level it is the continuing business of assigning time and staff to the many different subjects and activities on the timetable, and devising the means to keep staff informed of new ideas and techniques. At classroom level (or 'departmental' level) it is the work of selecting and connecting sequences of lessons, and the important process of determining the content of these lessons. The term *curriculum management* is sometimes used in relation to the responsibilities of school managers. But to 'manage' the live interactive process which makes curriculum is to effect change, since curriculum must change continuously to be always relevant to changing

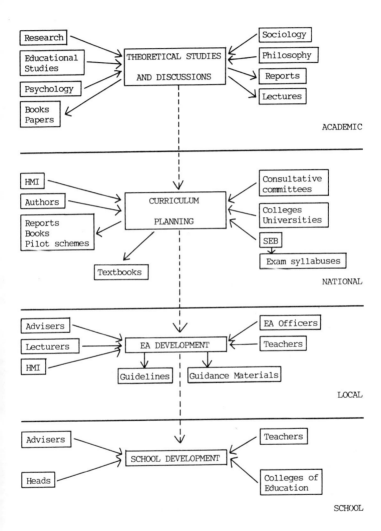

FIGURE 1: Levels of curriculum development

circumstances. For that reason *curriculum development* seems a more accurate term. Thus we have *development as statement, development as dissemination,* and *development as school management.*

6. Curriculum statements

A curricular statement leads to development at all levels. This is what spells out the educational principles which underlie any proposals for change. A 'packaged' curriculum tends to consist of a statement of aims and principles followed by detailed guidelines for particularised class groups, often accompanied by outlines of content which may also comprise model lessons. It was through curriculum packages that most of the subject developments of the 1960s and 1970s were achieved, and all of the advanced education systems in the world have employed this method on a large scale. The production of packages has indeed become something of an industry, and at national level governmental bodies, university and college project teams and teams of teachers at regional level have achieved considerable productivity over the last 20 years. In Scotland the Standard Grade and National Certificate development programmes have relied heavily on curriculum packages.

7. School programme

The production of what is called here a school programme is a continuous process in all schools. The term *programme* is used in this context because it signifies more than just the formal curriculum; it can represent also the informal curriculum and various features of organisation which, though not recurrent, are designed to contribute to it, for example, Founder's Days, sports meets etc.; the term can also include the school's arrangements for staff development, future planning, staff consultation etc. There have been some radically new school programmes proposed from time to time—for example, project-based schemes for primary schools and task-oriented schemes for the early secondary stage—but generally in Scotland the school curriculum has its basis in established arrangements of subjects and schemes of activity, and innovations are introduced piecemeal and with caution.

The timetabler uses last year's timetable and adapts it to change arrangements or make room for additional elements. In essence, the evolution of new activities and approaches in the scheme of things at school level must be regarded as the 'purest' form of curriculum development, not only because it is this which most potently changes pupils' learning but also because it is this which most effectively influences teachers' attitudes and professional behaviour. The introduction of new or improved curricular elements into departmental or classroom syllabuses will often begin from the dissemination of packages produced at national level, but it is only when these have been assimilated by the school—that is, recognised, made room for and resourced—that they become properly established. As Gordon Kirk says, 'curriculum development is precisely what enterprising teaching is all about'.[12]

8. Models of dissemination

There have been many studies of the different methods whereby innovations are spread and adopted in an organisation. Models of dissemination have been described which can easily be applied to curriculum development. The literature throws up some colourful accounts, for example of the 'Johnny Appleseed' model in which an individual promulgates new ideas by visiting institutions, or of the 'contamination' model whereby ideas are conveyed from one 'convert' to others, or of the 'cascade' model which requires the 'conversion' or 'formation' of a cadre of leaders who pass their wisdom on to a larger group who repeat the process with a yet larger group and so on. It is not really useful to teachers to study the philosophy of dissemination, since the models as theoretical constructs tend to disintegrate in the light of practical experience; but it may be helpful for persons engaged in curriculum development to be aware that there *are* different operations to be seen at work.

The most significant distinctions are probably those between the centre-periphery method and the self-generating method—that is, development by a leader group and passive reaction by the majority on the one hand, and on the other hand development by the members of an organisation for their own institutions. Another distinction is that between a top-down model and a bottom-up model. 'Top-down' implies a superordinate leadership acting upon subordinate personnel. 'Bottom-up' implies that people at 'grass-roots level' initiate and carry through the development for themselves.

All of these methods are insufficiently precise to yield useful pictures of how curriculum development actually occurs in an education system. It is commonly assumed that development in Scottish education is top-down, centre-periphery and authoritarian in character, but in fact the picture is much more complex than these terms suggest. The processes of curriculum development occur at all levels in the Scottish education system, and practising teachers are involved in significant ways at every level. It can be claimed with some justification that there are both top-down and bottom-up forces at work. At the same time there is a long tradition of top-down and centre-periphery development which is scarcely ever challenged.

REFERENCES

1. Kerr, John F., quoted in *The School Curriculum*, by W. Kenneth Richmond, Methuen 1971.

2. *Curriculum Design for the Secondary Stages* issued by the CCC 1987.

3. MacBeath, J., *Personal and Social Education*, Scottish Academic Press, 1988.

4. Rodger, I. A. and Richardson, J. A. A., 'The Organisational Implications of School Self-Evaluation' in *School Organisation*, Vol. 4, No. 2. 1984.

5. Mackenzie, R. F., *The Unbowed Head*, EUSPB, Edinburgh 1978.

6. Richmond, W. Kenneth, *The School Curriculum*, Methuen, 1971.

7. See Gordon Kirk, *The Core Curriculum*, Hodder and Stoughton, 1986.

8. Issued by the Scottish Education Reform Committee in 1917.

9. *Secondary Education: A Report of the Advisory Council on Education in Scotland*. Cmd 7005. HMSO 1947.

10. *Primary Education in Scotland*. HMSO 1965.

11. *The Structure of the Curriculum in the Third and Fourth Years of the Scottish Secondary School*. HMSO. 1977.

12. Kirk, Gordon, *Teacher Education and Professional Development*, Scottish Academic Press. 1988. p. 5.

CHAPTER 2

THE GROWTH OF CURRICULUM DEVELOPMENT AT NATIONAL LEVEL

1. *The Scottish Education Department*

In so far as curriculum development may be said to have occurred at all before the middle of this century, it was the responsibility of the Scottish Education Department (SED) and the various bodies vested by the Department with authority to offer it advice. A succession of education Acts beginning in 1872 made it clear that, although school boards (and, later, local authorities) were charged with the duty of 'providing' education in their schools, it was the government which had the power and the means to introduce and control changes in curricula. The Department's officials, both the 'administrators' like the Secretary and his subordinates and the 'professionals' in the Inspectorate, were actively engaged over many decades in shaping and reshaping the ideological framework from which the curriculum emerged. It is clear from the literature that there was a continuing and often vigorous discussion of the objectives of education and the best means of realising them in the schools.[1]

Even after the institution of Advisory Councils from 1920 onwards the Department was the principal source of curriculum control and development. It was the codes and circulars issued from the SED which determined the shape and content of school curricula, and it was its inspectors who ensured that its decrees were implemented. His Majesty's Inspectors advised the local authorities about their education schemes and officially

approved them; they oversaw the award of school certificates at every level; they set the examination papers for
the Leaving Certificate, marked the scripts and conducted
the crucial oral examinations in schools; during the 1920s
and 1930s they 'came to exert full pressure upon the
secondary curriculum and methods of teaching' and
'exercised great authority in elementary schools, influencing everything that was taught. . . .'[2] They appear to
have done little positive curriculum development in the
1930s, but they had some influence on the Advisory
Council's Report on primary education.[3]

During the 1950s the Department published a number
of memoranda, on the primary school curriculum, on
various secondary school subjects, and on junior secondary education. These were written by HM Inspectors
and their recommendations formed the major curricular
concerns for the decade. In the late 1950s, under the
powerful leadership of John Brunton, the inspectorate
began to develop a strong, positive attitude to curriculum
development. He encouraged inspectors to put forward
more progressive ideas about courses of study in the
secondary schools and he set about reorganising the
examination structure. The new fourth-year Ordinary
Grade gave schools the impetus to introduce courses more
suited to the needs and capacities of the less academic
pupils, and inspectors played a prominent part in helping
to design new courses. During the 1960s the Inspectorate
took on a new role, their inspectorial function giving
way to a strong leadership in curriculum development.
Brunton and his senior colleagues appointed 'particular
bright young inspectors' to introduce new ideas, new
teaching approaches, and new attitudes in the schools.[4]

The 1955 report on Junior Secondary Education was
the last major work on curriculum produced entirely
within the SED. In the late 1950s Brunton and the
Secretary of SED, Sir William Arbuckle, achieved the
establishment of Working Parties whose membership

included educators from outside the Department. Reports by working parties of this kind could obtain a greater degree of trust from the profession, and their recommendations were likely to win support from a wide range of interested groups. It was such a working party that produced the important introduction of Ordinary Grade examinations. Other influential working party reports were *From School to Further Education* (1963), which was known as the Brunton report because he acted as chairman, and *Primary Education in Scotland* (1965), known as the Primary Memorandum.

Individual inspectors' methods of developing curricula changed radically during the 1960s. During the first half of the decade the established procedures were followed: panels of inspectors, one for each subject, produced internal memoranda to be used by officers in their routine visits to schools. Armed with new notions, HMI would talk about them to teachers, sometimes even demonstrating a new approach in the classroom. Innovatory approaches might form the basis of an official report which would be included in the Blue Book (the Secretary of State's report to parliament) and sometimes reprinted as a pamphlet. Some pioneering inspectors, however, began to discuss new ideas with directors of education and with their help they formed local groups of subject teachers to study and experiment with curricular innovations. In the larger education authorities, particularly Glasgow and Edinburgh, teachers began to get time off school to sit with an HMI and produce new schemes for teaching their subjects. In one or two subject areas inspectors collaborated with Colleges of Education to mount national summer courses, and these proved to be important sources of seminal innovation.

With the great institutional reforms of the mid-sixties— the establishment of the Scottish Certificate of Education Examination Board (SCEEB) and the Consultative Committee on the Curriculum (CCC), some inspectors assumed an overt leadership in the management of curriculum development. Senior officers sat on the SCEEB and CCC, and individual inspectors sat on the new central committees alongside lecturers and teachers. A few individual inspectors took on a public leadership role in curriculum development which was unprecedented.[5]

During the 1970s the inspectorate's leading role in curriculum development diminished. The CCC and its many central committees and working parties took over the major tasks of producing and promulgating new ideas and proposals; inspectors, of course, continued to be influential members or assessors in committees. With the publication of the Munn and Dunning reports and the government's decision to reorganise examinations and courses on the basis of their recommendations, the central and decisive role of the inspectorate was re-emphasised. It was the Department's central development unit, staffed by inspectors and officers of SCEEB (now SEB, the Scottish Examination Board) which initiated and controlled the production of the new Standard Grade courses. By the mid-1980s, however, the majority of the inspectorate were fully engaged in formal school inspection, which had been reinstituted by the government. While curriculum development has continued to be an important element in the work of HMI, the current emphasis of the inspectors' role lies more in the implementation of curricular policies through their examination and analysis of the work of schools.

2. *Advisory and consultative bodies*

The provision for an Advisory Council on Education in Scotland made by the 1918 Act was a gesture towards allowing more professional and public participation in the process of forming policies. Since two thirds of the members were to be drawn from bodies with educational interests, and the Act stipulated that the SED should 'take into consideration' the advice of the Advisory Council, the first council set up in 1920 was welcomed as a salutary counter to the rigid centralist control which has long been characteristic of the Scottish system. It had been apparent that the Department was 'out of touch and at odds with significant Scottish opinion' on many issues.[6] But the SED was not disposed to allow the new Advisory Council and its successors much scope. It was not until the Sixth Advisory Council (1942–47) produced its outspoken recommendations for change that there developed a widespread recognition in Scotland that there could be an effective alternative to curriculum development by the SED. The Advisory Council's proposals were, of course, merely advisory, and their recommendations were addressed to the Department. Yet although the Council's leading members were disappointed at the profession's apparent unwillingness to challenge the Department's hostility to reforms, this Council's proposals did give 'fresh impetus to progressive thinking'.[7] According to Sir James Robertson, the chief writer of the report on secondary education, those who were concerned with education as a social service welcomed the proposals while those with a narrower professional interest were 'noticeably cooler'.[8]

In its chapter on the Inspectorate, the secondary report commended the inspectors' developing role as 'consultants and collaborators' rather than inquisitors, and the Council recommended that inspectors should do less routine inspection and 'devote their time to more constructive functions'. These functions were described rather vaguely: 'to stimulate by discussion and suggestion, to spread ideas and be a link between school and school, to provoke the unreflective to thought and to awaken healthy doubts as to the sufficiency of familiar routines. . . .'[9] Although the senior chief inspectors, Watson and Pringle, 'objected very strongly to most of the suggestions that were made about the Inspectorate', according to Brunton, he and other less senior officers were profoundly influenced, and when Brunton set about reorganising the Inspectorate and gave the ordinary ranks a voice (after he succeeded Pringle as SCI in 1955) there was a growing consensus in favour of less formal inspection and more work in curriculum and staff development. Officers like Dickson, C. A. Forbes, Shanks, Emond, Fullwood and Bennett supported Brunton's policies, and younger men like McGarrity, Chirnside, A. K. Forbes, W. K. Ferguson and A. J. Mee carried them out at district level. By the time the last Advisory Council ceased to meet (1961) there was a receptive climate in the SED to the introduction of consultative agencies with authority to participate in curriculum development. Among the seventeen new recruits to the inspectorate in 1961 and 1962, at least eight could be described as a 'new breed' of innovators, determined to change the curricula of Scottish schools and colleges by injecting new, up-to-date content, by moving schools towards progressive approaches, and above all by setting themselves up in partnership with college lecturers, researchers and teachers for the production of new curriculum programmes.[10]

3.   The CCC

A Glasgow teachers' strike has been said to have caused the SED to set up a Consultative Committee on Educational Matters (CCEM) in 1961–2, but the move was clearly in accord with the policy of Arbuckle and Brunton to promote a greater degree of cooperation between the Department and its 'partners' in the running of the education system—the EAs, the professional institutions and the teachers' associations. The CCEM's remit was to act as a 'forum for discussion of general policy on educational matters, particularly those affecting curricula, examinations and school organisation' and its membership was to be drawn from the constituent bodies on a delegacy basis. Both the comprehensive nature of its remit and its apparently 'democratic' constitution were incompatible with the SED's style of government, and the CCEM soon dwindled to the status of a casual Liaison Committee, while its remit was divided up among the new bodies such as the SCEEB and the CCC.[11] Interestingly, the CCEM, had it been allowed to develop, would have resembled the Schools Council in England and Wales (and would doubtless have suffered the same fate at the hands of the Thatcher government in the 1980s).

The CCC was set up in 1965. It was a new phenomenon in Scottish education, being a kind of standing working party, with membership changing every four or five years, solely concerned with the curriculum. Its concern with the curriculum as a whole was also new: not since the Sixth Advisory Council in the 1940s had there been a mechanism for reviewing the whole curriculum. It was in keeping with the relatively recent growth of professional curriculum theorists that there should be an official means of examining the relationships between subjects and school activities in the constitution of the whole curriculum; subject specialists (as were all HMI concerned with secondary schools) might become, it was thought, too obsessed with the importance of their own subject, 'demanding or postulating amounts of school time that just cannot be there if a balance is to be held'.[12]

There can be no doubt that the CCC was carefully designed to be purely advisory in status, and that its work was to be wholly controlled by the SED. The Secretary of the Department assumed the chair, and at every meeting he was flanked by as many as ten officers, both inspectors and administrators, who acted as secretariat and assessors. All the two dozen or so non-SED members were handpicked and officially appointed (by a letter personally signed by the minister) 'as individuals on the basis of their personal knowledge and experience rather than as representatives of particular organisations'.[13] In its first years of existence it was run on a shoestring (as Graham admitted to the Parliamentary Select Committee in 1968). Compared to the Schools Council south of the border, it was tiny and powerless. It was also, on the face of it, unrepresentative, its members being wholly independent of their normal employers and professional associations. But the membership was selected to be representative of the Scottish education system: it included headteachers, college of education principals, university professors and directors of education. The inspectors played a powerful part in raising questions, discussing issues and reporting back the results of enquiries.

Unlike the Advisory Councils, the CCC did not work at a remove from the SED. It could no longer be said, with the same accuracy, that the committee proposed and the Secretary of State disposed; for the Secretary of State's chief education officer sat in the committee's chair, and his presence there assured the CCC of a direct voice— if not in actual decision making then certainly in the formation of policy. Of course in most matters dealt with by the CCC the ministers responsible for Scottish education took no personal interest; thus although the name 'the Secretary of State' was solemnly invoked in committee discussions, when the chairman said he thought the Secretary of State would agree to such-or-such he meant that he himself would undertake the appropriate action. The CCC was, in effect, the SED sitting in conclave, with attendant advisers, to debate various proposals for the curriculum. Since it met only three or four times a year as a body, its policies were formulated by *ad hoc* working groups or sub-committees, and its intentions for change were enacted through published reports.

The first CCC's remit was to maintain a general oversight of the curriculum, to bring to the Secretary of State's notice any curricular topic requiring special attention by a working party, and to comment on the recommendations of working parties.[14] It contented itself initially with setting up sub-committees and working groups (which included persons who were not CCC members) to produce draft reports on specific topics, such as the introduction of metrication and teaching about decimal currency in primary schools. At about the same time as the establishment of the CCC the Department set up the Central Committee on English (CCE) and a national working party on the new subject of Modern Studies. These were not, as has been mistakenly recorded here and there, 'panels' or sub-committees of the CCC. They were at first wholly independent creations by the SED. By the time the Central Committee on English had prepared its first Bulletin, however, the CCC had assumed authority to 'call it in' and discuss it prior to its being approved for publication by the Department. Out of this procedure developed the practice that became the regular means for the production of curriculum development packages: a central committee or national working party—set up by the SED sometimes, but not always, on the CCC's recommendation—would produce a report: this would be discussed and approved (sometimes after subsequent drafts) by the CCC; and the SED would publish it through Her Majesty's Stationery Office (HMSO).

By the early 1970s the CCC was producing a number of important curricular studies and consultative documents. In the period 1971–74 it had working parties on Classics, Health Education, Computers, Physical Education, Technical Subjects; it had a group studying the problems of transition from school to university; and it had a sub-committee looking at the 'Communication of Aims in Secondary Education'. In addition there had been published, under the CCC's auspices or by the SED on its recommendation, reports and memoranda on English,

Modern Studies, Science, Community Service, Art, Technical Education, Primary School Mathematics, Modern Languages, the Social Subjects, the raising of the school leaving age, nursery education and coordinated courses for girls.

In 1974 the CCC consisted of a main committee and its secretariat, with a quite massive substructure of sub-committees and *ad hoc* working groups. The Central Committees (now all called Scottish Central Committees (SCC)) were now all virtually accountable to the CCC. There were central committees on Primary Education, English, Modern Languages, Science, Social Subjects, Technical Education; a Secondary Mathematics Committee and a Committee on Mathematics for General Education; a working party on Drama; a working party on Music; a Scottish Computer Education Group; and a working party set up to investigate the best organisation of the school day, week and year.[15]

Although the CCC was a non-statutory body, it had been set up by the Secretary of State with a full awareness of its potential importance as an official advisory committee. By 1974 there could be no curricular proposals of substance emanating from the SED that had not first been discussed, amended where it was deemed necessary and approved by the CCC. Because of its high status its operations were described to each succeeding minister, and of course with any change of government its remit, composition and structure would have to be reviewed. For this reason the 1971–74 CCC was continued in office until 1976. During these two years it set up new central committees on Physical Education, Religious Education and Mathematics; it approved Central Committee reports on English, Modern Languages, and the Social Subjects. Most importantly, it recommended the setting up of a committee to review the curriculum of the third and fourth years of secondary education—the Munn Committee which reported in 1977. From its inception, however, the CCC remained very much a subsidiary agency at the SED's command: it had limited and uncertain authority in respect of the many central committees and national working parties; it had very little control over the publishing of major reports through HMSO; above all, it had no control over the budget assigned to it by the SED.

4.   The New CCC of 1976–80 and 1980–83

As a result of an internal review by the Department, the new CCC of 1976 was given new powers and a new structure of committees and development centres. Its remit was widened. It was now not only to keep the curriculum of schools under continuous review; it was given control of existing central committees and empowered to set up its own working parties and central committees, to decide their terms of reference and supervise their work; it had control over the selection of membership of its sub-groups and the allocation of funds for its many projects; and it was free to publish whatever it wanted under its own auspices. Most of these powers were subjected to 'the agreement of the Secretary of State', but the presence of chief SED officers on the CCC ensured that that would be a matter of course after the committee had arrived at a decision. The operational procedures could, for the most part, be carried on without reference to ministers.

The most important feature of the new CCC structure was that it assumed ownership of what is now called the Scottish Curriculum Development Service (SCDS). This had its origin in 1967 with the setting up by the Central Committee on English of CITE, the Centre for Information on the Teaching of English. The CCE had persuaded a number of EAs to set up local Development Committees (LDCs) and wanted a national centre to collect and disseminate materials. CITE was set up by

Moray House College of Education with the somewhat reluctant agreement of the SED, and it was almost wholly due to Tom Brown, head of English, and the principal, Dr. Douglas McIntosh, that it could be staffed by a secretary and a librarian, with Brown acting as Director. The idea of a national centre for developing the subject became attractive to other central committees, and in 1971 there appeared the Scottish Centre for Mathematics, Science and Technical Education in Dundee College of Education, the Scottish Centre for Social Subjects in Jordanhill College of Education, and the Scottish Modern Languages Centre in Aberdeen College of Education. A Primary Education Support Service (PESS) was set up in 1975. Hitherto these centres had been virtually independent of the CCC. The 1976–80 CCC created the SCDS by reorganising and extending the structure of development agencies which had grown up piecemeal.

The new CCC structure initiated in 1976 is illustrated in Figure 2. The business of the CCC was prepared and conducted by the Steering Committee, which was chaired by A. D. Chirnside, H. M. Depute Senior Chief Inspector of Schools. Chirnside, in close collaboration with J. A. Mitchell, Secretary of SED and Chairman of the CCC, and Miss P. A. Cox, Assistant Secretary of the SED, was the principal architect of the complex new structure. Sitting with him on the Steering Committee were John Ferguson, rector of Fraserburgh Academy, John Macleod, depute director of education in the Highland Region, Keir Bloomer, a prominent member of EIS, Professor Jack Standley, University of Dundee, Dr. John Walker, Director of the Examination Board, and the author, who was then Chief Adviser in Lothian Region. This group was an epitome of the Scottish education system: while they were in no sense vested with representational authority the members could variously bring forward the views of the government, the inspectorate, the headteachers, the teachers' unions, the directorate,

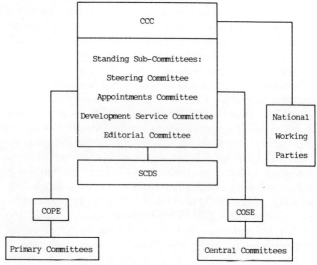

Figure 2: The CCC Structure 1977–1980

the universities, the Examination Board and the advisorate. This was effective not only in shaping an agenda
for the main committee but also in persuading the committee to accept their recommendations for action.
Another important group was the Appointments Committee: chaired by Ian Flett, director of education in Fife
and also Secretary of the Association of Directors of
Education in Scotland (ADES), it was able to consult a
wide range of bodies in seeking suitable members for the
innumerable central committees and working parties.
The Development Service Committee coordinated the
complex management of the curriculum development
centres. The Editorial Committee designed and managed
a new arrangement of curriculum papers, reports, discussion papers and information leaflets, the main one being
the 'CCC News' issued to all schools and centres.

Two new major sub-committees were established. The

Committee on Primary Education (COPE) carried on the work of its predecessor, the Scottish Central Committee on Primary Education, but it had a closer relationship to the main CCC and was given parity of status with the new overarching Committee on Secondary Education (COSE). These committees, for the first time, concerned themselves with the development of curriculum in their sector on a comprehensive basis. Each had a strong bias in favour of positive action. It was no longer satisfactory merely to set up working groups and publish their findings: COPE and COSE set about the creation of a national network of research and development agencies assigned to bring about lasting curricular changes. They adoped the policy of involving teachers in schools as much as possible in their work. Newly formed central committees would henceforward always have a majority of 'practising teachers', though in practice, for an obvious reason, most of these had attained some promotion in their jobs. The obvious reason was that the Appointments Committee could only seek nominations from established bodies such as the EAs and the inspectorate, and it is not surprising that the nominating persons tended to recommend people who had won their attention. By 1980 several hundred Scottish teachers were engaged in curriculum development work at national level.

The division of the CCC's policy making function into COPE and COSE suggested that certain aspects of the curriculum should be the concern of special deliberative committees. The most important of these was COSPEN (the Committee on Special Educational Needs), first constituted in 1980 under the chairmanship of Magnus More, then First Depute Director of Education in Fife. The COSPEN membership comprised members of the main CCC and of COPE and COSE. Its principal function was to coordinate the efforts of the whole CCC structure in developing the curriculum required for all pupils with special educational needs. COSPEN's work was both theoretical and practical. It was the first national development agency in this field, and through its newsletters, conferences and published materials it quickly effected important progress in the improvement of curricula for handicapped pupils. COSPEN continued to be an important part of the CCC's structure until 1987, and despite the omission of special educational needs from the list of priorities commended to the CCC by the government's Crawley Review it can be expected that COSPEN's role in some form will continue to be upheld by the new SCCC.

The CCC had hitherto been serviced by the SED: administrators at the rank of Principal Officer and below attended meetings, kept minutes, arranged for correspondence, saw to the payment of expenses and so on. The new CCC of 1976–80 was given its own permanent secretariat. An HM Inspector, David McNicoll, was seconded for this purpose and given a small full-time administrative staff. This was an important development, since it not only gave the CCC a greatly more efficient administration but it also gave it a measure of independence from the SED proper—both in respect of action and in status. The Steering Committee could now have its decisions acted upon without recourse to lengthy consultations within the SED.

5. Working parties

The CCC constituted a convenient device for satisfying demands for major investigations and projects in education. Ministers and others who wanted 'something to be done' about any particular problem which related to the curriculum could be assured that the CCC would be asked to take it up. Thus once it had been established as the country's major development agency the CCC's agenda always included what came to be called Special Projects and Development Programmes; some of these were set up at the request of the SED and some were initiated within the CCC itself—but all were, of course, approved by the SED before they got off the ground. The procedure was much the same for every project: a small planning group would devise a remit, estimate costs and likely duration, and draw up a formal proposal; appropriate persons would then be invited to sit on the governing committee, a secretariat and chairperson would be appointed and the committee would then begin its work. Its remit would require it to report to the CCC at given dates; otherwise, the project would proceed with virtual independence, setting up enquiries, project groups, conferences and pilot experiments as it saw fit and was able to fund from its assigned budget. When its final report to the CCC had been approved, sometimes after considerable revision and amendment, it would be submitted to the Secretary of State and eventually there would be a governmental statement of the Secretary of State's views and decisions.

The Munn Committee, which began as a subcommittee of the CCC of 1971–4, was the creature of the CCC itself, but its report, published in 1977, represented the most important changes in Scottish secondary education through two decades. Its chairman, James Munn, a member of the 1971-74 CCC, became the longest serving chairperson of the CCC (from 1980 to 1987) and by virtue of that position (and his own personal ability and charm) was later given the chair of the Manpower Services Committee and a knighthood. The report of this committee became a lengthy preoccupation of the whole Scottish education system and it was one of the CCC's central tasks to transpose its propsals into practical curricular programmes. The Munn Committee proper was constituted early in 1975 and its membership was fairly representative. It included four headteachers, two assistant headteachers, three principal teachers, two college principals, a university professor, an EA adviser, an EA education officer, the director of the SEB, the depute director of the Scottish Council for Research in Education (SCRE), and the head of the Education Department in Jordanhill College: thus it represented, unofficially, almost every section of the education system which dealt in any way with secondary education. It was mainly a deliberative body, undertaking no development work, but it consulted widely by holding three residential conferences and taking evidence from a large number of persons and groups.

Because it was recognised that there was a close—some would say integral—connection between curriculum and assessment, the Munn Committee had 'discussion and exchange of information at all stages' with the Dunning Committee on Assessment.[16] Both reports were deliberately published at about the same time; and all the consequent curriculum development arising from both reports was undertaken by joint working parties appointed severally by the SED, the SEB and the CCC. This approach to curriculum development, both in the initial process of identifying aims and approaches and in the later stages of devising teaching programmes and piloting courses in schools, has become the standard practice in Scotland where more than one of the governmental organisations are involved. It is a satisfactory arrangement because it brings different forms of expertise to bear on the work; it does, however, have what many consider to be the disadvantage of depending solely on the SED for its funding, management and leadership.

A different form of curriculum development was adopted for the project on 'Education for the Industrial Society' (EISP). This was set up in 1977 in response to the then Labour government's call for a review of education's contribution to the economic growth of society, and in particular to the urging of the Parliamentary Under-Secretary of State for Education (Frank McElhone) that schools should do more to prepare pupils to play their part in bettering industrial relations. It suited the SED admirably to pass the responsibility over to the CCC, and a joint committee of the CCC and the Department's Scottish Committee for Schools/Industry Liaison was appointed to prepare a remit and development programme.[17] A Project Planning Committee (PPC) was set up, comprising both educators and industrialists, and this set about planning and establishing an elaborate network of study groups, experimental projects, commissioned researches and consultations. In the course of six years' work the PPC produced more than twenty reports on different aspects of the secondary curriculum, all of them prepared by committees of teachers and representatives from the many industrial firms who cooperated with the EISP. Its final report, *An Education for Life and Work* (1983) was a comprehensive discussion of the whole secondary curriculum, with suggestions as to how a concern for developing the vocational education of pupils can permeate the curriculum and blend with the principles of a general, liberal education for all.[18]

As is often the case with long-standing projects, the EISP had by 1983 become a central element in the work of the CCC, and the PPC's recommendation that a Scottish Education/Industry Committee (SEIC) be set up was readily accepted by the then (Conservative) Minister for Industry and Education. The SEIC has survived various economy drives and has effectively implemented many of the curricular innovations proposed and piloted by the EISP. Work-related studies of various kinds are now integral to secondary school curricula, and the work of EISP and SEIC (albeit hugely strengthened by the incentive offered by government through its TVEI (Technical and Vocational Education Initiative) schemes) must be recognised as one of the most successful curriculum development programmes in our educational history.

The 'Education 10–14 Programme' was a major curriculum development project initiated and funded
entirely by the CCC. It was not a response to political
demands but a consequence of the CCC's own deliberations on the education process. An interesting feature
of its origin is that a 'Starter Paper' on 'Education of the
10–14 Age Group' was produced by a joint committee of
COPE and COSE and disseminated throughout the
whole education system in 1980. This was in effect an
invitation to EAs and others to review their provision for
these pupils and let the CCC know whether they supported its belief that there should be a major project
to develop new solutions to the problems besetting the
primary-secondary transition. The system's response was
greatly in favour, and a Programme Directing Committee
(PDC) was set up in 1982. Its membership was charac-
teristically representative: the chair was taken by D. G.
Robertson, Director of Education of Tayside Region and
a member of the main CCC; there were two primary
heads, two secondary heads, three secondary principal
teachers, a depute secondary headteacher, two primary
advisers, two secondary advisers, a college of education
lecturer, the depute director of the Scottish Council for
Educational Technology (SCET)—George Paton, for-
merly principal of a college of education and an authority
on primary education; two chief inspectors of schools—
and a parent. The PDC was 'coordinated' by S. B. Smyth,
Director of the Edinburgh Centre of the SCDS, and his
Principal Curriculum Officer for primary education. The
development methodology adopted by the PDC included
the now standard procedures for CCC projects: a survey
of EA provision and activities was put into operation;
one group set out to produce a 'rationale' which set out
'a theoretical basis for a 10–14 curriculum'; a second
group analysed and evaluated the information received
from the survey and consultations; a third group devoted
itself to analysing research literature. An important inno-

vation was that the PDC's remit required it to 'arrange for such feasibility, pilot or research studies as may be required . . . to be undertaken by Education Authorities or any other appropriate bodies or individuals'.[19] Unfortunately the work was seriously frustrated by the disastrous industrial dispute of 1984 to 1986 which led teachers to boycott cooperation in curriculum development. Thus an excellent curriculum development model—which should have enabled the PDC to describe actually achieved experiments in its 1986 report—was badly weakened. In the event, however, the report, *Education 10–14 in Scotland*, was a brilliant and important discussion of the 10–14 curriculum on the basis of which much curriculum development work still remains to be done.

Several other working parties were set up. A project on 'Micro-electronics, Computing and the Curriculum' (MCC) (1981–83) set out to create a curriculum for 'computer literacy'.[20] A 'Scottish Resources in Schools Project' (SCOTRES) (1982–85) defined needs for Scottish studies in the curriculum. A project on 'International and Multicultural Education' (IMEP) (1982–86) contributed valuably to this area of curriculum development, although it was local authorities such as Lothian and Tayside which achieved the most significant advances in this field.[21] Other working parties oversaw such initiatives as the Equal Opportunities for the Sexes Project (1983–86), the Scottish Development Programme in the Expressive Arts in the Primary School (1984–87), the Foundations of Writing Project (1981–86), and the Social Subjects S1–S2 Programme (1983–86).[22]

6. *The SCDS*

The 1976–80 CCC set about reorganising the curriculum development centres and drew them together under the title Scottish Curriculum Development Service (SCDS). As the CCC was busy setting up a comprehensive range of central committees—its object being that no subject or main school activity should be without a national development committee—it decided that the development centres should serve the whole of the CCC structure. Each centre was expanded in its scope. The Modern Languages Centre in Aberdeen was closed in June 1982. By the end of 1983 a new SCDS was operating in three centres, now called the SCDS Glasgow Centre, the SCDS Edinburgh Centre, and the SCDS Dundee Centre.

The Glasgow Centre was now responsible for Business Subjects, Classics, Guidance, Home Economics, Religious Education and Special Educational Needs as well as the Social Subjects. The Dundee Centre was responsible for Art, Computing, Mathematics, Nautical Subjects, Technical Education and Science and Technology. The Edinburgh Centre took over the Primary School Service responsibilities for Environmental Studies, Expressive Arts, Home/School/Community Relationships, and Language Arts. Its secondary school responsibilities were for Drama, English, Gaelic, Modern Languages and Physical Education. This clustering of subjects and curriculum areas was arrived at by a combination of expediency—to suit people who lived in an area—and logic, so that officers' special knowledge and skills could be exploited. The same might be said of the allocation to the centres of responsibility for major development programmes: the Glasgow Centre took on the work for 'Education and Industry' and 'Education 16–18'; the Dundee Centre took over 'Microelectronics, Computing and the Curriculum', 'Tour de France', and the work of the Committee on Technology. The Edinburgh Centre took on 'Education 10–14', 'Needs of those with Mild or Severe Mental Handicap', 'Application of Microelectronic Technology to Primary Environmental Studies', and 'Foundations of Writing in the Primary

School'. Each centre also assumed the management of one of the national support services which the SCDS had developed. Glasgow had the Audio-visual Service and the Evaluation Service; Dundee had the Publications Service and a library service for Mathematics, Science and Technical Education; Edinburgh had the Language advisory and library service and the publishing of the two prestigious journals, *Teaching English* and *Modern Languages* in Scotland.[23]

The service is still being managed through three separate but closely coordinated centres, but now has its headquarters in Edinburgh. There have been some attempts over the years to persuade the CCC that a single national centre should be developed. There are several important arguments in favour of this move. Besides the obvious economies of staff and other overheads that would ensue, it would achieve a more powerful organisation with more effective impact on schools. It would facilitate the coordination of the efforts of different experts and make an integrated curriculum more feasible. It might be allied to a national staff college which would coordinate curriculum and staff development with research and perhaps the development of new assessment methods. Above all it would present a single, more easily perceptible identity to the schools. Against these arguments may be posited disadvantages pointed out severally by officers and CCC members. Besides the cost of disrupting and reorganising well established centres, a move towards centralisation would reinforce the suspicion that centralisation meant great political control. The distribution of the service among three geographical areas means that it is more likely to attract the support of local authorities. Teachers are able to attend and work at the centres more economically. The loyalties and goodwill built up by each centre over the years would be lost. Above all centralisation would mean the loss of support to the individual centres of the colleges of education which housed them. Whatever the merits of these last arguments against a single national centre, the SCCC and its officers have so far successfully resisted the efforts of politicians and administrators to centralise the SCDS.

REFERENCES

1. See, for example, Scotland, J., *The History of Scottish Education*, vol. 2. ULP 1969; Bone, T. R., *School Inspection in Scotland*, ULP 1968; Knox, H. M., *Two Hundred and Fifty Years of Scottish Education 1696–1946*, Oliver and Boyd, 1953; McPherson, A. and Raab, C., *Governing Education*, Edinburgh University Press, 1988.

2. Bone, T. R., *op. cit.* p. 185.

3. See the report, *Primary Education* (Cmd. 6973. SED. 1946. p. 14)

4. Bone, T. R., *op. cit.* pp. 227 ff, McPherson and Raab, *op. cit.* pp. 86 ff.

5. Report from the Select Committee on Education and Science, *Part II. Her Majesty's Inspectorate (Scotland)*. HMSO. 1968. p. 26.

6. McPherson and Raab, *op. cit.*, p. 48.

7. McPherson and Raab, *op. cit.*, pp. 247 ff.

8. Robertson, J. J., in the *Scottish Educational Journal*, 12 April 1957.

9. *Secondary Education*, HMSO. 1947. pp. 139–40.

10. See Bone, T. R., 'The Changing Pattern of School Inspection in Scotland' in *Scottish Educational Studies*, vol. 1, No. 1, June 1987.

11. See McPherson and Raab, *op cit.*, for a comprehensive analysis of SED policies at this time.

12. Norman Graham, Secretary of SED, in *Report from the Select Committee on Education and Science*, HMSO, 1968, p. 25. Graham was the first chairman of the CCC.

13. Third Report of the CCC, 1971–4. HMSO. 1975. p. 5.

14. First Report of the CCC 1965–68. HMSO. 1969.

15. See the CCC Third Report, 1971–74. HMSO. 1975.

16. *The Structure of the Curriculum in the Third and Fourth Years of the Scottish Secondary School*. HMSO. 1977. p. 7.

17. For a full discussion of EISP and its work see A. Douglas Weir, *Education and Vocation 14–18*, Scottish Academic Press 1988.

18. *An Education for Life and Work*, CCC, 1983.

19. *CCC Fifth Report, 1980/83*, 1983.

20. *CCC Fifth Report, 1980/83*, 1983, p. 37.

21. See MacBeath, J., *Personal and Social Education*, Scottish Academic Press, 1988, for a discussion of the relationship between anti-racist ideas and social education.
22. For reports on these projects see the *CCC Sixth Report 1983–87*.
23. *CCC Fifth Report*, Dundee College of Education 1983, pp. 116–7.

CHAPTER 3

THE CCC IN THE 1980s

1. *After Rayner*

The Thatcher government has required two major reviews of the CCC and the SCDS: the first in 1980 (the so-called Rayner Study) and the second in 1984–86, the Crawley Review. In keeping with the government's policy to reduce public expenditure and to dismantle as many quangos as possible, the Rayner study set out to question the complexity of the CCC structure and the cost involved in maintaining it. It was suspected that the SED offered the CCC to Rayner as a tethered goat. Be that as it may, the CCC was the first Scottish quango to be investigated by the prime minister's inquisitor. It emerged with a measure of triumph from the review, and the report, *Curriculum Development in Scotland*, firmly endorsed the value of the CCC.[1] It agreed that the CCC 'should continue to take responsibility for services which might more appropriately be provided by education authorities, colleges of education, or even associations of subject teachers'.[2] It has been observed that this important question was never followed up, perhaps because the SED did not want to question the relative contribution of parts of the education system other than itself.[3] At any rate, the government reiterated its intention to employ the CCC in its *Statement* later in 1980.[4]

The report suggested changes which would reduce the complexity of the CCC structure and effect some economies. It proposed that COPE and COSE should consist only of CCC members, thus changing them from

large representative bodies to small executive panels of
the main committee. This was resisted stoutly by the
CCC and subsequently the government accepted that
they should continue to include non-CCC members. At
the same time, all the committees were to be reduced in
size. A more economical use of inspectors and officials
was intimated; henceforward there would be only one
HMI and one SED administrator on the CCC, and
COPE and COSE would have one HMI each: all these
officers were to be assessors, not full members. A major
departure was the appointment of an 'outside' chairman:
for the first time, the CCC chair would not be occupied
by the SED Secretary but by a lay nominee. This change
was not at first well received by the CCC, as it was felt
that the old arrangement symbolised its national and
official authority. The new chairman, James Munn, was,
however, a popular choice, as he had been a CCC member
since 1968 and had chaired the influential Munn Committee. Another welcome decision was to widen the membership by bringing in persons from industry and parents'
bodies.

As we have seen, the 1976–80 CCC had rationalised
and extended its network of sub-agencies, set up COPE
and COSE, and ensured that their sub-committees should
always contain a majority of teachers. The Rayner Report
suggested that, in the interests of economy, there might
be fewer subordinate bodies and that committees need
not necessarily exist for all subjects at all times. It proposed that the Steering and Appointments Committees
should be replaced by a chairman's Executive Committee, which should have more authority to take action
on behalf of the main CCC. The CCC agreed that its
substructure should be slimmed down, but decided that
it would continue to maintain a comprehensive range of
specialist committees. It agreed to institute the powerful
Executive Committee. The Rayner Report proposed that
the SCDS should be reduced in size and its organisation

modified with a view to locating all the staff ultimately in one centre. The CCC began to study the case for centralisation and took the important step of establishing its Secretary, David McNicoll, as the head of SCDS. The directors of the Centres were all appointed to COSE and the director of PESS to COPE. The Rayner Study, according to Humes, 'could hardly claim to have been a startling success' in the light of the government's policies: it achieved very little in the way of economy or greater efficiency.[5] But the CCC itself regarded the outcomes as highly satisfactory. The Report and the Secretary of State's Statement both constituted a strong endorsement of the CCC's aims and activities and promised it continuity in support and status. One CCC member had this to say:

'Scots may not have much of a reputation for compromise, but I think the CCC represents a veritable masterpiece. It still has all the status and prestige of the SED behind it, not least those of HM Inspectorate. This enables it to recruit a vast reservoir of time and energy; hundreds of educators work hundreds of hours per annum for it in their own and their employers' time. Yet it manifestly operates independently, increasingly being seen to have its own claims to authority and loyalty. It can be insistent in its guidance without being directive, comprehensive in its concerns without being too bland. It has achieved a central place in the scheme of things, but it calls on and receives the support of almost every organised educational body in Scotland. It manages its own considerable budget and has never had real cause to complain about the amount; yet its resources are provided by a benevolent State department; above all its officers—the secretariat and various field officers—are provided free by the SED with all their high ability and wide experience. It can react to problems quickly, reach decisions without long-drawn-out politicking and implement its plans with relatively smooth efficiency. It may not exactly look like this to Scottish teachers—or even to its own members—but the more one sees of comparable national bodies the more one feels ready to settle for what it is.'[6]

In the years following, the rather high-flown self-satisfaction indicated in that passage had to be considerably modified. There were two forces now strongly at work in the SED: one was the new assertiveness of the government in its determination to implement its policies; the other was a corresponding pressure on the CCC to become less of a policy-making body and more of a functionary agency required to implement the government's policies. Writing in 1985, Humes pointed out that 'CCC activity has, increasingly, been heavily circumscribed by government initiatives: the Munn/Dunning Development Programme, the 16–18 Action Plan and the Youth Training Scheme have all reduced its room for manoeuvre'.[7] In subsequent years this has become all too evident. At the first meeting of the 1983–87 CCC it was made clear that the 'main energies' of the organisation would be absorbed by major development programmes initiated by the SED and 'priorities' such as the rationalisation of the curriculum, technology in the curriculum, social education and 'translation of curriculum theory into effective classroom practice'.[8]

When the Secretary of State decided in 1980 to implement the SED's modified version of the Munn and Dunning proposals for curriculum and assessment for S3 and S4, the SED set about adopting what the CCC admitted was 'a leadership role'[9]: a Departmental Development Unit, managed by an Assistant Secretary and four chief inspectors, set up 32 Joint Working Parties (JWPs) to devise new courses. SCDS and SEB officers worked with inspectors and seconded teachers and lecturers on these JWPs and they reported to Steering Committees chaired by inspectors or examination board officials. The seconded teachers acting as Development Officers were located in the SCDS centres, and most of the full-time secondary staff of the centres were used in the designing and piloting of Standard Grade courses.[10] In keeping with the government's policy of concentrating resources for its own programmes, the central committees began to be discontinued in 1984: thus in 1986 the CCC decided to replace the 17 subject-based central committees by a smaller number of 'deliberative' committees of a 'cross-sector and cross-disciplinary' nature. In future it would also set up short-life working groups (known colloquially as SHOLIWOGS), a device of the SED's Development Unit, and these would undertake special studies and tasks for a prescribed period of time. The disappearance of standing central committees with a high measure of autonomy and their replacement by *ad hoc* and tightly controlled groups was another instance of the increasingly apparent trend towards centralised control which has been a salient feature of curriculum development in the 1980s.

2.   *After Crawley*

By 1986 it was agreed in both the SED and the CCC that some radical changes were necessary in the CCC's functions and structures. The CCC produced 'Proposals for Reorganisation of the CCC Structure from August 1986' and the SED delegated an Assistant Secretary, D. J. Crawley, to assess the organisation and propose changes. The Crawley Review was very much an administrator's assessment: it was blunt, shrewd and practical. Its major criticisms suggested the need for 'tighter discipline' over publications, with a 'more commercial approach', 'further rationalisation of the committee structure', improvement of 'management' and 'accountability'. Members of the CCC should continue to be 'appointed on a personal basis' but the balance of membership should be adjusted in favour of teachers and 'the community'. EA members should be included 'in the light of their functional responsibilities within education authorities as well as their potential personal contribution'. The CCC's remit should continue to require it to advise the Secretary of State and to give guidance to authorities and schools; and 'it should work within clear priorities'.[11]

The Crawley Review reflected a number of the Thatcher government's educational preoccupations. It proposed a considerable reduction in the CCC's resources: 'rationalisation' of the committee structure would result in reduced expenditure and less teacher control of development: 'tigher discipline' would increase the powers of the central planning committees and the SED; improvement of 'management' would have the same effects of reducing costs and increasing control. A 'more commercial approach' would obviously reduce the CCC's capability of influencing the education system by requiring it to concentrate on publications with marketable potential, and it would (and did) spell the doom of prestigious but heavily subsidised publications like *Teaching English* and *Modern Languages in Scotland*.[12] Greater 'accountability' clearly meant accountability to government, not to the whole education system. The 'priorities' to be set are obviously to conform to the government's policies. At the same time, the Crawley proposals also reflected some of the CCC's own concerns for closer association with teachers, EAs, schools and society at large, and for a more synoptic approach to the curriculum, enabling it to free itself to some extent from the influence of 'subject lobbies'. Cross-disciplinary committees could view the curriculum with a more eclectic appreciation of the needs of pupils and society rather than the academic demands of the subjects. The CCC could promulgate an understanding of 'curriculum' which has long been sadly lacking in Scottish secondary schools, though well established in the primary sector: that is, of the curriculum as expressing the educational intentions of the whole school rather than an aggregate of the aims and approaches of separate subjects.

The government's decisions on the recommendations of the Crawley Review, and the CCC's response to it, were communicated in a letter from the minister to the CCC chairman in March 1987.[13] Although he reiterated the government's recognition of the value of the CCC, he announced a number of 'radical changes in the way the CCC and the SCDS operate'. The most radical change which emerged was that, on the Thatcherite principle of 'value for money', the whole enterprise would be established as a 'company limited by guarantee' (as had been suggested by Crawley) on 1 April 1988. The precise implications of this change remain unclear, but the government evidently felt that it would resolve 'anomalies' in the relationships of the CCC with the SED and with the SCDS and the colleges of education: it would set up a 'clear and logical basis of operation' separate from the colleges, and it would remove any possible element of autonomy from any of the SCDS centres. The creation of an integrated organisation for curriculum development under the management of a Chief Executive is clearly an attractive proposition. From the government's point of view, this distancing of the CCC from itself has the advantage of giving it an apparent independence of status, but at the same time the CCC's total dependence on the SED for funds and members will make it even more amenable to the control of the SED.

The new Scottish Consultative Council on the Curriculum was set up as a company limited by guarantee and not having a share capital under the Companies Act of 1985. The objects for which the government set it up were carefully described in a Memorandum of Articles of

Association drawn up in the SED with the help of the
Scottish Office legal department. These are as follows:

(1) To keep under review the curriculum of schools in
    Scotland and to advise the Secretary of State for
    Scotland as to any matter relating to such cur-
    riculum.

(2) To promote, carry on and keep under review a
    programme of curriculum development work in
    accordance with policies, programmes and priorit-
    ies agreed from time to time with the Secretary of
    State. In this work the SCCC is expressly enjoined
    to 'liaise with the education authorities, schools
    and any other bodies and individuals whom the
    Council considers are likely to contribute to the
    development of the curriculum.'

(3) To issue guidance on the curriculum to education
    authorities and 'such other agencies as the Council
    considers are likely to benefit from or require such
    guidance'.

In carrying out these objects the Council is under
explicit instructions to 'have regard' to certain con-
straints: principally, 'current economic and social
concerns', the need to 'develop and strengthen' relationships between school education and training and employ-
ment; and 'the implications of the Council's advice for
the use and priority of resources allocated to school
education by schools, education authorities and central
government'. It was clear from the beginning, therefore,
that the SCCC was to be a governmental device for
the implementation of its curricular policies. The SED's
control was emphasised in various memoranda and
guidelines associated with the Articles. The SED was to
pay grant to the SCCC in each financial year, and the
availability or amount of grant would be decided arbi-
tarily by the Department. Any moneys not spent by the
Council are to be forfeited and failure to use funds would

affect future grants. The SCCC would be obliged to submit estimates and forecasts, along with accounts, and these are to be studied in the light of 'priorities' agreed between the Department and the Council. The Council is required to seek SED permission to enter any commitment exceeding £5000. Its accounts are to be audited in the normal manner and the grant payable would be subject to regular monitoring throughout the year.

All these limitations are normal in respect of any governmentally funded enterprise, and they constitute no significant change from the arrangements developed for the former CCC. But in other respects incorporation effected much greater financial autonomy for the new Council. It would be free to apply for and receive additional funds from any suitable source, such as the European Community or local authorities or companies or private individuals. (No doubt the SED grant might, of course, be reviewed in the light of such transactions.) It would now be free to make grants for research and development projects, employ freelance agents of any appropriate kind, acquire any properties or equipment it needed, invest money, support any other institutions with grants, and in general act with the powers of any normal incorporated body. None of these powers had previously been available to the CCC. No doubt the SCCC will continue to be severely controlled by the SED and its officers: but no doubt, too, its day-to-day freedom from the SED bureaucracy will give it much greater scope for action in the fulfilment of its objectives. The paraphernalia of business company legalism which surrounds the Council's incorporation should not hide the fact that its separation from the Department's official organisation gives it a new potential for effective curriculum development.

The Secretary of State continues to control the membership of the new Council. Although they are governed in their work by a Board of Directors (drawn from the membership), they are in effect still strongly led by the SED. All the members are appointed by the Secretary of State and subject to his control in respect of the duration of their service. He determines the size of the Council and its composition. He appoints Assessors. He appoints a chairman. He is under no constraint whatsoever as to the kind of person he appoints, the professional or social representation of the membership, or the number of any particular group. On the other hand the Council is free to appoint any committees it wants, to select the conveners, and to determine the membership of its committees. Its Board of Management, comprising the chairman and not less than five members of the Council, has extensive powers and responsibilities.[14]

The membership of the SCC appointed in September 1987, like that of its predecessors, is to a large extent representative of the various sections of the Scottish educational system. There is a nursery school head and three primary heads. There is a primary adviser and an adviser in Guidance. Six members are secondary heads, and one is a depute head. There is a head of a special school with rural experience. Three members are from EA directorates, two being directors and one responsible for a large advisory service. There are two university professors, both with experience of serving on school-related committees. Two are principals of colleges of education. One is principal of a Further Education college. One is an educational psychologist. The chairperson, Sister Maire Gallagher, is an ex-headteacher and a distinguished member of previous CCCs and other national bodies. The political predilections of the government are no doubt reflected in the fact that of thirty council members no fewer than five are persons whose experience lies in industry and commerce rather than education. Two members are representative of parents' organisations, symbolising the government's policy of giving a stronger voice in education governance to parents. It has been openly alleged that the minister's political prejudices led him—soon after the general election of 1987—to exclude members of the EIS from the SCCC.[15] It is not true that there are no EIS members on the Council. But like all its predecessors, the SCCC comprises persons who have been selected by SED officials, in consultation with the minister responsible, as individuals likely to contribute valuably to its work—in the eyes, of course of the SED—and it is the case that none of the EIS's nominees were selected.

The reconstitution of the SCDS under the new Chief Executive has effected little change. The SED's proposal to centralise the operation in a Dundee Centre was frustrated by what amounted to a rebellion among Council members and their officers, but few believed that the retention of the *status quo* would be permanent. The SCCC's three centres, now called 'offices', remained in Glasgow, Edinburgh and Dundee. The four senior posts in the SCDS were changed. There were now two Directors of Curriculum Development, one for 'design' and for the 5–14 age range, and one for 'evaluation' and the 14+ age range. There was a Director of Policy and Administration and a Director for Information, Marketing and Publications. An office manager was appointed to run each centre. The SCDS functions were distributed among the offices on a basis of convenience for the staff; and the Edinburgh office, which houses the Chief Executive's office, is regarded as the headquarters. Figure 3 shows the new staff management structure.

From the point of view of the education system it serves, the day-to-day operational autonomy of the new SCCC must be welcomed. It will, it is hoped, develop into a more 'accountable' organisation because it will be more dependent on the acceptability of its services to EAs and schools. It will increasingly work in close cooperation with the directors of education and their staff, especially with local authority advisers and curriculum devel-

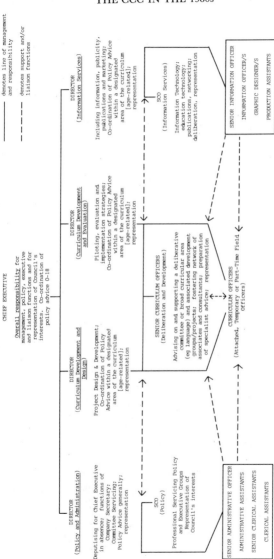

Figure 3: The staff management structure of the SCCC

opment officers. It will increase its capability of gen-
erating funds, and no doubt this will result in a greater
measure of autonomy; but it will have to guard against
the ever present danger of arbitrary financial bullying
which all quangos are subjected to by aggressive politicians. There seems little prospect of the SCCC's escap-
ing from its subjection to the SED; but there is every
prospect of its being able to adopt a more independent
line of curriculum thinking than has been manifest in
recent years. There can be no doubt that the SED sees
its main job as converting government policies into educational strategies, and converting its educational thinking into school programmes and materials. The Council
may be required to implement a national curriculum
framework and to design it in accord with the politicians'
views, putting forward a plausibly attractive educational
rationale for ideas that may be in themselves crude and
professionally unacceptable. On the other hand it will
continue to be able to initiate new ideas and express its
professional opinions to both government and public. It
is explicitly prohibited by its charter from publishing
reports that have not been approved by the SED. On the
other hand it has the power to object, openly and publicly,
to any policies it cannot itself approve. Many Scottish
educators will continue to deprecate its lack of autonomy
and the arbitrary nature of its provenance and management, but it now has an opportunity to win the trust
of the education system and prove its usefulness. New
political developments may well occur to enable the
SCCC to develop into a more representative, more professionally accountable institution: if and when that may
happen, the model of curriculum development it has
created in recent years should prove itself to be educationally effective and socially powerful.

3.   The national model of curriculum development

Figure 4 demonstrates the considerable complexity of

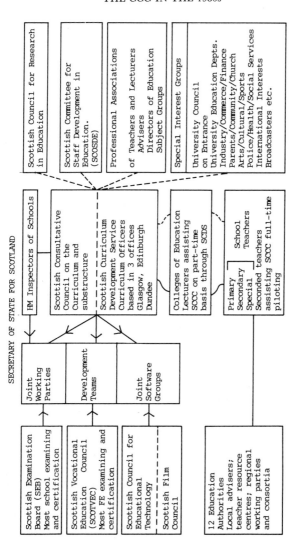

Figure 4: Organisation for Development of Curriculum

the organisation which has grown up in recent years to produce the modern curriculum. Almost every educational body which exists has a role to play in the design and framing of curriculum. The Scottish Examination Board (SEB) is a statutory body set up in 1963 to provide external examinations leading to national certificates at school level. Although its functions exclusively concern the assessment of pupils at the end of their day-school careers—at S4, S5 and S6—the syllabuses it produces for its examinations virtually control the curriculum for S1, S2 and S3 for the simple reason that teachers tend to perceive the examination requirements as the principal determinants of the content of their programmes of work. The SEB has subject panels for every examined course, consisting largely of specialist teachers. This has been seen to give a measure of democratic control to the Board: but in both the Board itself and in the subject panels the SED, mainly through the Inspectorate, has a strong and influential presence. It has been argued that the SEB is firmly controlled by the SED[16], but between the formation of general policies on assessment and the actual design and content of examination syllabuses lies a good deal of practical curriculum development which is the work of the Board's officers and the many teachers it employs.

It can happen, unfortunately, that the examinations officers' contribution to the design of a curriculum is malign. For example, a curriculum which is designed to be 'pupil-centred' and 'task-based', and consequently dependent mainly on being assessed within school by the teachers may have to be changed to provide separately assessed elements and a marking scheme to suit the general guidelines set down by the SED.[17] More frequently, fortunately, the SEB's involvement in curriculum design enables a course to be methodically organised and therefore more effectively taught and assessed. The Joint Working Parties set up to bring together the staff of the SED, the CCC and the SEB in the work of devising courses for the new Standard Grade certificates were clearly more efficient than separate groups could be, given that courses must be assessable as well as teachable. The close relationship between curriculum and assessment is now universally acknowledged, and it has been suggested that for all practical purposes there would be merit in the amalgamation of the SEB with the SCCC to create a Board for Curriculum and Assessment, such as exists, for example, in Australia.[18] But curriculum development must never be dominated by the requirements of formal assessment: much that is educationally valuable would be lost from many courses if they were to be forced into the Procrustean bed of an external examination.[19]

The Scottish Vocational Education Council (SCOTVEC) is, like the SEB, an institution for the awarding of national certificates and the provision of assessment procedures leading to the award. It was set up in 1985 to implement the government's 'Action Plan' for rationalising all non-advanced further education courses and awarding a single National Certificate in place of the former plethora of different certificates and diplomas. In the designing of the modular courses which make up the new curricula for further education, SCOTVEC's officers and the teachers, lecturers and researchers they employ play a strong development role; and the fact that their modules are now widely available at school level produces a strong influence on the secondary curriculum. Even before its inception, there was talk of merging SCOTVEC with the SEB: and the vision of a single, governing body for all externally controlled certification and assessment is still an attractive one for many Scottish educationists.[20]

The curricular functions of the Scottish Council for Educational Technology (SCET) are limited to courses in which modern technological equipment is appropriate. It has played a leading part in the development of computer education and in the utilisation of computers throughout the primary and secondary curriculum. It has pioneered and greatly assisted the development of software for numerous courses in many subjects. It has played a leading role in the production of a curriculum in Media Education, comprising studies of films, TV, etc. both as elements of the curriculum and as vehicles of instruction.

The Scottish Council for Research in Education (SCRE) is the most important of all the bodies coexistent with the SCCC in the realm of curriculum development. Its establishment in 1928 was in itself an attempt by the local authorities and teachers' associations to provide a national source of educational thought and development.[21] Curiously, however, despite the close connection between research and development—symbolised by the use in industry and science of the familiar term 'R and D'—there has been little genuine cooperation between the SED and the CCC on the one hand and SCRE on the other. Most of the projects undertaken by CCC groups contain an element of 'research', in the sense that they employ techniques of surveying, analysis and evaluation, but they have seldom actually employed professional researchers.

The colleges of education have played an important role in the history of curriculum development in Scotland. College principals have figured in the CCC from its inception, and lecturers abound in its numerous planning and development groups. It was the colleges that made possible the setting up of the SCDS and they kept them going until the establishment of the SCCC. Much of the work of central committees, local development groups and research projects owes its provenance and management to college staff.

The university departments of education have produced a large number of research studies, books and discussion papers on curricular subjects, and the dissertations produced by their post-graduate students constitute a fruitful, if largely unharvested, body of work. Few major national committees have not included a university scholar in their membership; some have been successful and stimulating conveners.

The Education Committee of the Convention of Scottish Local Authorities (COSLA) contains some of the most powerful politicians in the country, and some of its officer advisers (members of EA directorates) are among the most knowledgeable and influential of our educators. Yet COSLA has failed to be a force in national curriculum development: it seldom discusses curricular matters, although it provides an official response to every major national report: it has never found the means to connect itself formally to the CCC or any other important body, although its members or advisers abound in their sederunts. Now that the SCCC is on its new footing of semi-independence it will surely wish to enlist the support of such a potentially strong ally.

The Association of Directors of Education in Scotland (ADES) is another potentially strong body which has not made its presence felt as a national force in curriculum development. As with COSLA, ADES is consulted about everything that matters in Scottish education.

The Headteachers Association of Scotland (HAS), the Association of Head Teachers (Scotland) (AHTS), and the Association of Educational Advisers in Scotland (AEAS) are all also weak and ill organised as bodies with pretensions to a national voice in education. Although the HAS has taken some initiatives—notably the initiative in 1972 which produced the Pupil Profile[22]—it has seldom influenced curriculum development at national level. The AEAS has interested itself for many years in curriculum development, as its newsletters testify: but it has set up no national mechanisms for discussion or policy formation, and its division into narrow subject specialist groups has precluded any kind of synoptic view.

Of the other bodies which appear in Figure 4, little need be said. The teachers' professional associations generally maintain national committees on curriculum matters; in particular, the EIS has subject panels which meet to consider, for example, the SEB syllabuses and examination results.

4. *The new model*

In March 1986 the CCC Secretariat issued to members a 'blueprint' for the organisation of curriculum development. This had resulted from consultations in 1984 with 'all elements of the CCC structure'. The prolongation of the teachers' industrial action had delayed the report's completion, and by the time the CCC had had time to begin developing its new organisation it was faced with the Crawley Review and the government's decisions on its implementation. The model produced was constructed by the 'sixth' CCC for the benefit of the 'seventh' CCC: and although the new Council may not have embarked *simpliciter* on developing the model in all its details, the arrangements described in the SCCC's 'Guidelines Relating to Organisation' bear close resemblance to the 1986 model, albeit a new 'business' jargon has been adopted.

Figure 5 illustrates the complex network of relations the new Council has set out to maintain. The full Council is responsible for major policy issues. Its agendas are prepared by the Chief Executive with the Board of Management, which includes the Chairman of Council and the Conveners of the various 'Executives' and sub-committees. Thus the Board is effectively the focal point for all major policies and decisions. There are six to eight Board Members nominated by the Chairman and approved by the Council. The Board meets regularly with the Chief Executive, The Council Secretary and the SED's assessors, and it assumes responsibility for the

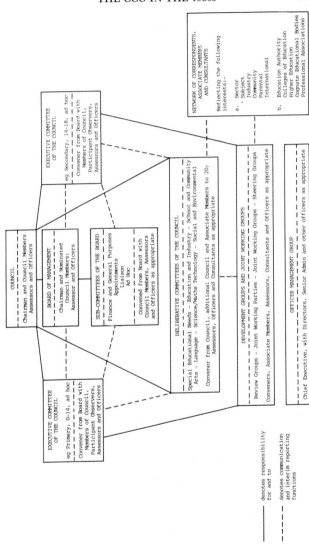

Figure 5: The 1988 SCCC Organisation

management of the Council's business, including matters of finance, accounting, property, staff, appointments and publishing. Board members also act as conveners of sub-committees dealing with finance and general purposes, appointments and liaison, and each has powers to convene meetings as required. An Officer Management Group comprising the Chief Executive, the four Directors and other officers, meets regularly to control the day by day management of all the Council's business.

The Chairman and the Board have set up Executive Committees to oversee curriculum development. These are the key functional groups, and they have high status, consisting of Council members and reporting directly to the full Council. At the time of writing (November 1988) there were Executive Committees for Primary 5–14 and Secondary, but the number of such committees will be determined by the Board as needs dictate. These committees are sub-groups of Council: the convener is a Council member, and the members (up to six in number) are all members. The Chief Executive is an *ex officio* member, as are the appropriate Directors. Importantly, an SED assessor (an administrator or HMI) sits on each committee, taking a full part in its affairs but not, by tradition, voting.

A number of Deliberative Committees has been set up to review aspects of curriculum and prepare guidance to EAs and schools. These are relics of the old Central Committees, and like their predecessors they are intended to represent the leading authorities in the curricular field they deal with. Normally each deliberative committee is convened by a Council member and includes up to 19 others, who are either Council Members or Associate Members. Each has a service group consisting of 'curriculum officers' and invited 'consultants'. In January 1988 there were Deliberative Committees on Special Educational Needs, Education and Industry, and School and Community. Further cross-sector committees were planned for Arts, Language, Science/Maths/Technology, and Social/Environmental matters. Thus an attempt has been made to ensure that the whole curriculum is being studied and developed. These Deliberative Committees will produce reports and proposals for development for consideration by the Council with consequent dissemination of guidance packages to EAs and schools. In addition, there are Development Groups and Joint Working Groups to which the Council contributes members and services. These normally have independent conveners and remits which emanate from the Council, or which are set jointly by the SCCC and the SED or other national agencies.

In pursuance of its instruction from the Secretary of State to work in cooperation with EAs and other interested bodies, the Council is establishing a 'network of Correspondents, Associates Members and Consultants': thus it can readily consult individuals and groups nominated by EAs, colleges of education, universities and further education colleges, professional associations and interested bodies. People from industry and commerce can be consulted or allowed to lobby the Council, as can groups of parents and community interests. In theory, anyone with any interest in curriculum may approach the Council with ideas, arguments, proposals; in practice, the Council is well equipped to cater for a very wide range of such interests. Whether it is well enough resourced to be able to deal adequately with all the work it has set itself has yet to be demonstrated.

REFERENCES

1. *Curriculum Development in Scotland: The Future of the Consultative Committee on the Curriculum and the Scottish Curriculum Development Service.* SED. 1980.

2. *Ibid.* p. 6
3. Humes, W. M., *The Leadership Class in Scottish Education*, John Donald, 1986. p. 87.
4. *The Consultative Committee on the Curriculum: Statement by the Secretary of State for Scotland.* SED. 1980.
5. Humes, W. M., *op. cit.*, p. 88.
6. Gatherer, W. A., 'Consultative committee on the curriculum—16 years on' in *Education*, vol. 158, no. 6. 7 August 1981.
7. Humes, W. M., *op. cit.*, p. 94.
8. *CCC Sixth Report 1983–87*, 1988.
9. McPherson and Raab, *op. cit.*, p. 320.
10. *CCC Fifth Report 1980–83*, p. 30; *CCC Sixth Report 1983–87*, p. 5.
11. The Crawley Review was published in mimeograph by the SED in 1986, and is summarised in the *Sixth Report of the CCC*, 1988.
12. *Teaching English* has continued to be published by a commercial firm, Macdonald Publishers, in association with Moray House College.
13. Published in the *Sixth Report of the CCC*, 1988.
14. Memorandum and Articles of Association issued to Council members during 1988, obtainable from SCCC, 17 St. John Street, Edinburgh.
15. See the *Oberserver Scotland* for 9 October 1988.
16. Humes, W. M., *op. cit.*, pp. 8, 85, 182.
17. See Mary Simpson's account, "School based and centrally directed curriculum development—the uneasy middle ground' in *Scottish Educational Review*, 18 (2), 1986, which describes how the requirements of the SEB for standardised procedures etc. destroyed the essential character of a curriculum in Health Education.
18. See Gatherer, W. A., in the *Times Educational Supplement Scotland*, 29 January, 1988.
19. See Gatherer, W. A., on 'School-based assessment versus external exams' in the *Times Educational Supplement Scotland, 15, 22 and 19 January*, 1988.
20. See Humes, W. M., *op. cit.*, pp. 184 ff. and Gatherer, W. A., in the *Times Educational Supplement Scotland*, 29 January 1988.
21. Wake, E. R., cited in McPherson and Raab, *op. cit.*, p. 257.
22. *Pupils in Profile*, SCRE, 1977.

CHAPTER 4

CURRICULUM DEVELOPMENT AT LOCAL LEVEL

1. *Responsibilities of the EA*

The EAs have always influenced curriculum development in the schools for which they are responsible, but until recent times they have done so accidentally, as it were, as a consequence of their policies for educational provision. At national level they are involved through their elected members and their officers in the work of the SED, the SEB and the SCCC; but these find themselves involved as individuals, without corporate attitudes or policies. It is at regional level, in respect of their own schools, that their influence is all-pervasive and decisive. In the broad sense of affecting the sweep of educational progress, the EAs have played a crucial role in the development of new curricula. In the 1960s the decision to develop comprehensive schooling had profound effects on curriculum, and it was the EAs who determined and brought about the actual curricular reforms that followed. In the 1970s it was the EAs who translated the reduction in the general level of educational resources into the logistical alterations which affected the curricula of schools: for example, reductions in ancillary staff, retrenchment in staff training opportunities and in the provision of teaching materials. In the 1980s it has been the EAs who have brought about curricular change in response to demographic changes and new governmental policies: changes in curricular provision resulting from falling rolls; new courses resulting from the Standard

Grade and Action Plan programmes, TVEI and other initiatives. In the 1990s it will be the EAs who meet the main challenges of further government initiatives such as the introduction of standardised testing and the imposition of national curriculum guidelines. All these changes in national circumstances require changes in regional provision which materially affect the curriculum actually delivered to schools.

Individual local authorities have in the past achieved radical changes in school curricula by adapting new policies of provision: for example, some EAs vigorously pursued a policy of building open plan primary schools, thus substantially furthering the pupil-centred curriculum; by enforcing mixed ability grouping in S1, some EAs brought pressure to bear on schools to develop the comprehensive school curriculum; by adopting TVEI proposals, some EAs have helped the rapid development of technology-biased curricula for S3 to S6 classes. But these initiatives have all been incidental in character: Scottish EAs traditionally have shown little interest in curriculum development as one of their prime functions. They have not substantially influenced the structure or content of the curricula in their schools.

The autonomy traditionally given schools in deciding what they should teach has been accorded them, by and large, by the EAs, not the national government. The SED has never neglected its responsibilities in respect of providing organised guidance to schools. Through the Inspectorate it has kept a keen eye on the curriculum for more than a century. The SCCC and its predecessors have owned their existence primarily, almost solely, to the SED. The tendency for national government to speak direct to schools reflects the traditional consensus in Britain, where local authorities have been regarded merely as intermediate enabling agencies rather than responsible agents of management. The law, however, thinks otherwise. Successive Education Acts have clearly vested the local authorities with the responsibility for providing a varied and comprehensive education service under the general guidance of the national Department. The Acts make it clear that it is the EA which is responsible for the 'adequate and efficient provision' of education, and explicitly indicate that this means responsibility for 'progressive education' appropriate to the 'age, ability and aptitude' of pupils. This means nothing if it does not assign prime responsibility for curriculum to the local authorities.[1] SED ministers and officers have, until recently, been meticulous in attributing the principal responsibility to the EAs, and this is explicitly stated in, for example, the reports of the CCC.[2] The guidance given out by the SED, through its inspectors, reports and approved CCC publications, has never been mandatory, though it has usually been directed straight at schools.

The anomaly of this relationship has frequently puzzled foreign observers of British education, but the general public, and particularly the press, do not allow themselves to be troubled by it. They assume, as do most teachers, that the SED is the prime source of curricular control. For example, when the minister of education pronounces his wish that a modern language should be a 'compulsory' element of the curriculum, the press feels able to report this as if a new law had been decreed.[3] But the fact is that the Secretary of State, while having governing powers over the whole education system, has always relied on the statutory obligations of education authorities to manage their schools, including the curriculum. His instructions regarding the implementation of regulations dealing with such matters as school buildings or health and safety are always issued to the local authorities. It is strange, then, that the guidance issued by his Department in relation to curriculum should almost always be issued to the general system, in the assumption that EAs normally delegate these concerns to the headteachers.

The EAs did not, for the most part, accept responsibility for curriculum development until recent years. They did not establish equivalents of the CCC or SCDS. They did not establish systematic arrangements for releasing staff to undertake curriculum development. They did not, in Scotland, provide formal means of assessing and reporting publicly on school curricula. They did not, for the most part, regularly publish information and advice to schools. They did not furnish resources for research and development activity. In each of these respects the SED has for many years invested greatly in effort and money. It is no wonder that the profession as well as the public look to the national government rather than local government for guidance on the curriculum.

It is not difficult to find reasons for this state of affairs. Traditionally in Scotland local educational management has been relatively small, powerless and apolitical. Curriculum for many decades was relatively stable, laid down in government instruments and accepted unquestioningly by schools, with little or no intervention by the local authorities. And when educational management came to be aligned with local political power after the 1930s, resources were so problematical that only persons of peculiar vision could occupy their minds with questions of curriculum. Most EAs were too small to be able to find the resources needed for local development until regionalisation in 1975; and even since then only the three or four largest EAs have been able to act in any significant way without government help. It was only with the formation of the larger regions that Scottish EAs were able to follow the longstanding examples of the great English metropolitan authorities and provide themselves with professionally competent curriculum development staff.

Local education authorities in Scotland are still too meagrely staffed to be effectively in control of curricula even if they wanted to be. In most EAs, few efforts have been made to provide the means simply because there has been no political will to have them. Elected members, even those of high intellectual ability and keen commitment, are seldom interested in the development of curriculum. Until comparatively recent times it was not expected of members that they should take an active interest in curriculum. Among Members of Parliament the situation is different. In 1981 all 79 Scottish MPs and MEPs were asked to state the areas of educational policy to which they would give special priority: out of 55 who returned answers, the curriculum was singled out of 11 aspects and given top priority by 23 members.[4] It is unlikely that a similar survey of local elected members would yield such a high interest in curriculum. Yet when officer-member (or member-officer) groups were formed in Strathclyde to consider educational topics there was genuine support from elected members. In Lothian, too, for some years a few elected members gave good service to Advisory Committees on different aspects of the curriculum.

It has been argued that it would be advantageous if EAs were to play a more significant role in curriculum development, on the grounds that in a democracy educational policies should be formed at the source of authority and that the EA is a major source of authority.[5] More effective curriculum development at local level would achieve a closer relationship between economic provision and curriculum. It can also be maintained that curriculum would be more effectively developed at local level, where there can be a more integral alliance between the planners at the centre and the implementers (the teachers) in the schools. As we shall see, in recent years the Scottish EAs have produced a great deal of curriculum materials, demonstrating how effectively that can be done at regional level. But if the EAs are to develop a greater capability for curriculum development, they would need to provide themselves with effective means. Curriculum development requires a study of the needs of pupils and the methods whereby teachers meet these needs. It requires a study of the community's needs and potentialities. It requires the continuous study of curricular theory and guidance, the designing of teaching schemes, experimentation, piloting, evaluation. EAs could, if they would, manage these processes more effectively than the national state agencies can—the question is, do they perceive themselves as being responsible and capable?

The study of pupils' needs ought to be a continuous process undertaken both at school and EA level: at school because it is there that pupils can be seen in the actual process of learning and at EA level because it is necessary to compare different categories of learning need, and no one school is likely to provide a sufficient range. This is work for teachers, but teachers engaged in such activity need time to do it: time free of pupil contact, time for training and practice (few teachers have the technical skills required of the researcher) and time for the actual process of assessment. Time would be needed to meet pupils and interact with them in different contexts; to meet parents and learn about relevant circumstances and preferences; time to meet colleagues who know the same pupils. Headteachers cannot provide these enabling conditions without the support and leadership of the education directorate, and heads themselves require continuous guidance on the management strategies required for this sort of activity. The EA is by far the best provider of the resources and guidance needed—perhaps the only readily available source.

To study the needs of the communities they serve, teaching staff need time and opportunity. Community relations can best be promoted when the EA encourages, authorises and resources it: the community schools developed here and there in Scotland have demonstrated the great potential of organisations designed to bring teachers into closer contact with the people for whom the schools exist.

There is ample evidence that parents welcome being invited to discuss curriculum, but it is important that they should understand its rationale. Without time specifically allocated to the teachers involved, this process cannot succeed. Teachers need to be trained to undertake this work, and they need opportunities to experiment, consult and review. For this the EA should be able to set up and maintain the administrative machinery for school/ community interaction, and this would be more effective if they appointed specialist staff to do the work. The introduction of School Boards will not succeed in helping teachers to develop a community-oriented curriculum unless the resources—including an acceptable apparatus for leadership—accompany the establishing of the organisation.

Above all, teachers need much more time to study curriculum in the form of curricular theory, reports of innovatory schemes, technical manuals and so on. The evidence of surveys of the extent to which such publications are actually read by teachers is sparse, but what there is is depressing. Even more depressing, however, is the manifest inadequacy of efforts to help teachers improve their knowledge and skills. The SED, the SCCC, the colleges of education and many other agencies work incessantly to encourage more widespread and intensive study of guidance documentation; but this activity is simply not built in sufficiently to the professional responsibilities of teachers. Headteachers do set up study groups, and advisers do organise courses, but EAs could do much more by recognising curricular studies as an important element of teachers' work, both because it is necessary for professional growth and because it is an essential feature of curriculum development.

2. *Mechanisms of EA development*

If the EAs are to give greater attention to their own responsibility for curriculum development, they must provide more specialist staff with the resources required. They should, for example, appoint a director of curriculum services with staff capable of carrying out the work. They should set up formal machinery for curriculum development, such as a sub-committee of the Education Committee, a research and development section of the administration, and standing consultative committees of teaching staff. Lothian's Regional Consultative Committees (RCCs) on primary and secondary education are examples of an organisation designed to supervise and promote curriculum development. Each is chaired by a headteacher and the membership comprises a range of administrative, teaching and advisory staff, with invited members—such as an HMI and lecturers from local colleges and the university. Vigorous efforts are made to ensure that the RCCs are fully representative of school staff: members are appointed by the Director from lists of nominees provided by the associations of headteachers and other staff categories. Serviced by the Advisory Service, the RCCs have an overview of the whole curriculum, and receive reports from a variety of study and project groups set up at their own instigation, often after being invited by the Director of Education to give advice on some topic. The RCCs meet regularly to discuss a range of business, including studies of curriculum undertaken by sub-groups or advisory committees. At one time or another, every aspect of the primary curriculum forms a subject of research and development, and practically every secondary subject has its committees and conferences; in addition *ad hoc* groups are established to produce guidance and recommendations on such aspects as personal and social education, multicultural education and education/industry liaison. Over many years the Lothian RCCs have, in effect, mirrored the national CCC in its concerns and operations, and they have proved useful points of contact between development projects at the different levels.

The machinery set up by Strathclyde is necessarily different given the different geographical character of the region. Each of the six area divisions has an education officer responsible for curriculum development and a team of Advisers and Staff Tutors to help in the processes of organising consultation, development projects and feedback. There are no standing consultative committees as in Lothian, but there are regular meetings of head-teachers. At regional level there is a Schools Sub-Committee of the Education Committee, a Depute Director responsible for curriculum and assistant directors responsible for different aspects of curriculum and staff development. All aspects of the curriculum are reviewed regularly by teams of officers, and working groups of different kinds are set up to produce new formations of curricular policies. Although the Advisers are deployed in the geographical divisions they meet frequently at regional level to review and develop curricular provision. This elaborate organisation of elected members, Directorate and Advisorate has proved to be highly effective in producing a comprehensive range of guidance, support materials and staff development activities.

All the Scottish EAs have established some machinery for curriculum development, but the lesser resources available to the smaller regions naturally constrain their efforts. Yet some of the smaller EAs have achieved impressive developments. The Borders Region, for example, has set up groups of teachers, Advisers and Staff Tutors to produce guidance on a wide range of topics, using Moray House College staff as consultants. By this means the Directorate have provided schools with a variety of curricular materials including documentation on Language, Drama, Environmental Studies and Computing. In Shetland, despite difficulties of travel and communication, impressive efforts have been made to use the professional expertise of teachers, particularly in the construction of common courses for the seven junior high schools which feed pupils into the only six-year comprehensive school.

Some EAs have undertaken large and sophisticated programmes of curriculum development. One of the most interesting was the Bilingual Education Project in the Western Isles. Partly funded by the SED, this project ran for six years, becoming in 1981 the Bilingual Curriculum Development Unit funded wholly by Comhairle nan Eilean (the Western Isles Island Council). In 1984 the unit was incorporated in the education department's Curriculum Development Service. A report on the first six years of the project was funded and published by the SED, the research having been undertaken by the Western Isles EA with financial backing from the inter-national Bernard van Leer Foundation. This was a community education project related to early education. The EA also undertook a two-year pilot project on the use of Gaelic as a medium of teaching in the secondary school.

In Dumfries and Galloway regional working parties organised by Advisers have produced reports and guidance documents on Music, PE, Learning Difficulties, Science subjects, Health Education, Modern Languages, Mathematics, Business Education, Computing; many curriculum packages have been produced for Standard Grade, TVEI and SCOTVEC courses. In 1988 a carefully articulated scheme of Staff, Curricular, Institutional Development (SCID) was launched. A document expounding the rationale for the scheme explains wisely that 'it seems illogical to deal with improving the courses and educational experiences of the pupils without considering how best to improve the teachers' own skills', and it sets out a framework of procedures for staff and curriculum development at the level of the individual, the school department, the whole school (or college) and the region. This programme, which has been generously supported by the regional council, points a way forward which will undoubtedly be emulated by other school systems.[6]

It will be evident from these examples that there is a wide variety of mechanisms for curriculum development at regional level. Each EA has evolved the machinery which best suits its own circumstances. There has been little direct cooperation among EAs to manage development: an interesting exception is Gaelic, the promotion of which has brought the Western Isles, Highland, Strathclyde and Lothian into partnership. Cooperative development work could well be extended, perhaps through COSLA and ADES, particularly if governmental pressures impel the local authorities to assert policies of their own. As things stand the SED is the only powerful agency which connects to all EAs, and its funds are, particularly for the smaller authorities, the only external source of support. The examples we have discussed also make it evident that EAs can be highly effective agencies for curriculum development. In a real sense the larger authorities could easily manage without the help of the SED or the SCCC: they have the resources and the leadership, and they have great authoritative status with the schools. But it is also evident that an integrated curriculum development service, bringing together the schools, the EAs, the SCCC, the SED and other national bodies, could constitute a very potent and effective machinery for development.

3.   Curriculum development at school level

It is a long established tradition in Scotland that the headteacher of a school carries the principal responsibility for the school's curriculum. This is true in the sense that the head is the manager of all that the school sets out to do; the head is responsible to the Director of Education, and through the director to the Education Committee, for what is taught, by whom the curriculum is delivered, and the standards achieved. This is not to say that heads actually design the curriculum *ab initio*, or that they have any real authority to make radical changes. But it is to the headteacher that people look—whether they be pupils or parents or teachers—for the many arrangements that go to make up the curriculum: the subjects or courses offered, the details of the timetable, the general peda-gogical approaches which make a dry plan into a live human process.

It is another long tradition, however, that heads them-selves generally feel that the curriculum is 'given' to them, in the form of accepted principles, attitudes and practices. No head is ever called upon to devise an entirely new curriculum: last year's timetable is the first and most powerful form of guidance available. Changes are proposed, usually, in the abstract—at national or regional level—long before they come to be taken seriously in the schools. The curriculum *is*, in an important sense, 'given': it is the creation of processes which are largely external to the school. Heads are expected 'to have regard not only to the instructions and guidance of their own auth-ority but also to the advice, the statements of policy or the decisions of various other bodies such as the SED, SEB, CCC and SCOTVEC'.[7] Yet it is the school, and not any other agency, that delivers the curriculum. The school has a four-fold contract for delivering the cur-riculum—to its pupils, to the parents, to the local auth-ority and to society at large as represented by the government, the press, the community and so on. In respect of each contractual obligation, the headteacher and staff have the duty to shape and express the edu-cational activities which constitute the curriculum. Thus the school must, inescapably, determine its own curricular policies and practices, based of course on externally imposed injunctions but essentially a very localised response to the staff's 'reading' of the demands of its four categories of 'clients'.

Although heads have a high degree of explicit responsibility in our system, another, more recent, expectation is that they will consult their staff on matters relating to curriculum. This is by no means a tradition in Scotland. So long as, over many decades, the curriculum consisted in the main of separate subjects, teachers were content to confine their attention—and their expertise—to the teaching of the subjects in which they were qualified; and heads were content to supervise a curriculum which was mainly a mere aggregation of subjects. Obviously, from time to time there came intimations from on high that certain new subjects were to be added—it was seldom that a subject was dropped—or that different emphases in teaching were to be looked for by the inspectors. Then the head would convey the new expectations to the staff and make appropriate adjustments to the timetable. But recent times have seen fundamental changes in curriculum which required important changes in school management. New emphases on the school's responsibility for the personal growth of pupils as well as their instruction in subjects have required the cooperation of teachers in adopting new techniques, designing new courses and exploiting new resources. In primary schools the 1960s saw a radical change in the very concept of curriculum which virtually removed instruction in 'subjects' as its main element. In secondary schools the recognition that society was changing its character and its requirements of schooling caused the appearance, during the 1960s and 1970s, of new subjects and new courses comprising elements of different subjects. The growth of Guidance as a school responsibility raised the need for pedagogical strategies that cut across the subject barriers and required complex new timetabling arrangements. The curriculum came to be seen ideally not as a list of separate subjects but as a programme of learning experiences.

In these circumstances the isolation of teachers in their subject departments was officially deprecated. Heads were now expected to hold regular meetings of staff: in secondary schools they were asked to consult the principal teachers on a regular basis, and the range of concerns expected to be discussed grew more and more extensive. The introduction in the 1970s of the new posts of assistant head teacher (AHT) greatly facilitated the process of consultative management. In primary schools it was customary for an AHT to be given responsibility for an age-group; in the secondary schools many AHTs were given functional responsibilities, and almost always at least one was given responsibility for the curriculum. This was by no means a universal feature, and many AHTs were uncertain about what they should be doing. But the presence of AHTs—often in secondary schools meeting with the head as a Board of Studies—advanced the more sophisticated perceptions of curriculum management and development which are nowadays held in the majority of Scottish schools.[8]

It is now held, widely if not universally, that all teaching staff should be asked to participate in the management and development of the school curriculum. This does not mean that the head's responsibility is diminished: on the contrary, it is expected that the head's management work will include arranging for staff to be consulted and involved in planning.[9] Teacher involvement begins in many secondary schools with regular departmental meetings, some of the business of which is consideration of the subject or course curricula, and the senior management team (that is the head, depute, and assistant heads) will often be represented. Meetings of guidance staff, interdepartmental meetings, *ad hoc* meetings to tackle a particular problem, or whole staff meetings are now normal. Some of the topics subject to professional scrutiny at such meetings arise from regional initiatives: examples from recent years are mixed ability teaching, multicultural education and 'area curriculum arrangements' whereby certain subjects are located in different schools and pupils are required to travel.[10] Ideally, however, a school should be continuously studying curriculum, and appropriate mechanisms should exist to enable staff to undertake this activity. Various arrangements have been used in recent years. All schools now have 'non-pupil days' when staff meet to undertake development work. Many primary school staffs meet once a week or so for discussion and exchange of information, in smaller schools all together and in larger schools in groups. A number of secondary schools have for some years developed a scheme of staff study groups which meet once a week when the pupils have gone home. These arrangements were formally approved by some EAs and grew into the 'Planned Activity Time (PAT)' suggested in the Main Report and later nationally prescribed. Unfortunately the amount of non-contact time made available for teachers is still grossly inadequate to allow them to undertake the kind of professional activity required, and the arrangements made in schools have been far from satisfactory.

The official expectations of headteachers' management of curriculum development are clearly demonstrated in HM Inspectors' reports on individual schools. In their accounts of primary schools they look for headteachers to provide guidelines on all aspects of the curriculum, and they commend the use of national and regional guidelines. They praise the production of internal 'curriculum policy statements'. They like to see 'termly plans' produced by teachers and 'policy papers' produced by heads. 'The Curriculum and its Organisation' is frequently reported on as a major aspect of the inspection. In their reports on secondary schools the inspectors want to see a school 'prospectus' or 'brochure' including a statement of the school's aims—or the aims of the head-teacher *for* the school. They commend a head's involve-ment in curriculum development at regional or national level. They describe various methods in use to help teachers participate in curriculum development: written papers exploring curriculuar issues; the formation of staff groups to study issues and propose new policies or arrangements; the deployment of senior promoted staff among teacher groups, or groups of departments, to study innovations and guidelines; sharing working papers among the whole staff.[11]

In this conception of curriculum development the head-teacher leads and manages; but some heads believe that their major duty is to facilitate staff-led curriculum devel-opment—to make arrangements for genuine school-based development by forming groups, providing time and materials, and organising consultative activities. It has been cogently argued that school-based curriculum devel-opment is the only kind that can genuinely succeed. Donald McIntyre writes: 'teachers have established a generally accepted right to autonomy, and a degree of privacy, in their classrooms, provided they meet certain minimal requirements such as covering specified syl-labuses, keeping the noise level down, and not assaulting their pupils.'[12] It is held that teachers cannot be forced to introduce innovations—certainly not in the ways required—and there are no 'teacher-proof' curriculum materials. Innovations will be accepted or rejected by teachers on the basis of their practical value. Externally directed changes will fail if they do not take sufficient account of the 'complex repertoires of classroom routines' on which good teaching relies.[13] School-based curriculum development, when sensitively managed and adequately resourced, brings much more enduring improvements in both the quality and the content of teaching. Sensitive management requires that there is a sense of 'ownership' of the innovations aimed at by the teachers who are going to adopt the changes. This means that the teachers must agree with the need for change and must accept the nature of the proposed change; ideally the teachers will have been personally engaged in developing the innovation, or in evaluating it. It means also that the efforts of the teachers involved should be overtly acknowledged by the appropriate authority, the head or the EA. Adequate resourcing means that time should be allocated to the work, that the necessary materials should be made available, and that the resources should be at the command of the developers themselves.

These conditions should enable schools to be mainly responsible for their own curriculum development even when the main thrust of change originates from outside. During the 1980s the SED's implementation of the proposals of the Munn and Dunning committees—or rather the government's own selection of proposals—followed a strong centralist line. In the name of maintaining standards, the SED and the SEB have used strategies of course development which, while employing teachers to work at national level, have barely acknowledged the schools' entitlement to choose and adapt approaches to suit their own needs. 'School-based development' has come to mean the piloting in schools of centrally produced courses, rather than development initiated or controlled by the schools themselves. In the past the schools have been able to assess for themselves the value of externally produced curriculum materials, and to decide whether or not to use them. This is still the case with regard to primary and early secondary courses; with regard to Standard grade courses, however, there is little of that freedom for schools. Courses are designed centrally and the SEB guidelines have the force of legal regulations; all that is left for teachers to do in their schools (or in regional EA groups) is to devise suitable materials for teaching the courses. There is now clear evidence of a trend towards

centralist control of the 5–14 age range. In modern parlance, curriculum development is top-down rather than
bottom-up.

But the relationship between development levels is
more complex than these terms seem to indicate. Courses
outlined at national or regional level may still be 'school-
focused' in the sense that they are designed mainly by
teachers, and development may rightly be called 'school-
based' in the sense that all the experimentation is done
in schools, and validated or amended as a result of
teachers' experience. This was the case with the S grade
courses on Social and Vocational Skills: pilot school
coordinators met regularly to devise the general course
outlines and guidelines, and the teachers involved felt
that the new courses were of their own making to suit
their own pupils. In the pilot schools themselves, suitable
mechanisms were constructed to make development
efficient: teachers worked in teams under a staff coor-
dinator, and had time and resources at their disposal.
Another multidisciplinary course, Health Studies, fared
less well because the SEB insisted on the imposition of
an excessively formal assessment scheme.[14] McIntyre
proposes a 'spectrum of perceptions' of curriculum development:

(1) not school based
(2) school based but externally controlled
(3) school based under teachers' control.

Either (2) or (3) can be effective, though McIntyre sees
(2) as 'burdensome' to teachers.[15] Simpson and Arnold,
the evaluators of the Health Studies development, distinguished between a 'participatory problem-solving model'
and a 'power model'. The former type is locally
controlled, responsible to local needs and drawing upon
local resources. The latter is directed by 'political leadership', with a 'clear administrative hierarchy for

decision-making'; it uses directives, rules and procedural guidelines; and it uses agents intermediary between the centre and the school to communicate central decisions.[16] There is ample experience to show that a 'power model' curriculum development project is bound ultimately to be less effective than a 'participatory model' project. The difference lies not in the provenance of the designed curriculum but in the methods used to develop it.

It is not to be supposed that the only sources of curricular innovation are the SED, the CCC or regional working parties. Many effective development projects originate from teachers themselves. In the early 1980s, for instance, some teachers of Chemistry in Lothian began to devise a new approach to the subject which they thought would give pupils more interest and stronger motivation to learn. Their new curriculum, 'Choice Chemistry', was developed partly in their own sparse spare time until they persuaded the EA to give them facilities to develop materials in bulk. Three teachers were seconded on a part-time basis to a teachers' centre and given the resources they needed, such as computer, word-processor, paper, printing facilities and travel expenses. Within a few years they had produced a new Chemistry curriculum which was adopted (and paid for) by a large number of schools throughout the country.

Curriculum development by individual teachers derives also from courses undertaken at universities and colleges. Many teachers taking the M.Ed. degree involve their own, and colleagues', pupils in innovatory activities. Many teachers taking a diploma in, for example, Learning Difficulties, devise and carry through a curriculum development project. As might be expected, most of this work ceases with the completion of the teacher's course, and much of the curriculum materials will disappear. But it can happen that a project undertaken in this way will influence the school in which the work was done substantively enough to make a lasting change. The teachers responsible are able to convey new curriculum knowledge and development techniques from the college to their colleagues, and their work can be ingenious and interesting. In the doing, too, the teachers are equipping themselves with expertise in curriculum development which will certainly benefit their schools.

The Robertson Report on Education 10–14 reiterated the belief that curricular review and management of change have to be undertaken by the teachers themselves, with help and support from 'support structures' within the school, in EAs and at national level. If maximum effect is to be achieved, teachers should be on the inside of curriculum development from the start. A balance must, of course, be achieved between 'the need for external support and guidance (and even direction) on the one hand, and teacher involvement (even control) on the other'.[17] The Robertson Committee proposed a collaborative structure for curriculum development, comprising coordinating teams within schools and, for each group of schools, a superordinate coordinating team which would set up working parties on different aspects of development work. Although it was devised for the development of a 10–14 curriculum, the model represents modern educational wisdom for all stages.

In his book *Teacher Education and Professional Development*, Gordon Kirk forcefully argues that curriculum development must be recognised as an essential feature of professionalism in a teacher. It is integral to effective teaching that it should involve planning and evaluation activities designed to produce a more effective curriculum. The now widespread acceptance of the view that curriculum development should begin in schools themselves accords with the perception of the teacher as researcher 'committed to the testing of curricular hypotheses in the classroom and the monitoring of the effects of different approaches'. The modern trends towards school-based curriculum development have 'strenghtened the professional autonomy of teachers and encouraged the rejection of practices which characterise the teacher as a low-level functionary dutifully implementing someone else's curriculum plans'.[18] Unfortunately more recent activities by government are in conflict with these liberal views.

REFERENCES

1. Education (Scotland) Act 1962 and Education (Scotland) Act 1969. Part I, para 1.
2. CCC Reports, 1965–68, 1968–71, HMSO.
3. See the *TESS*, 19 July 1988 which reported that the government 'announced its expected policy reversal on modern language teaching . . . making it compulsory for pupils to study at least one foreign language by 1992 in S3 and S4'.
4. *Speaking for Scotland, a Guide to the Social Policy Priorities of Scottish MPs*, published by the Scottish Council of Social Service, January 1981.
5. See Gatherer, W. A., 'The Local Education Authority and the Curriculum', *Education Policy Bulletin*, University of Lancaster, vol. 9, no. 2, 1981.
6. *SCID: Framework for Regional Policy* issued in April 1988 by the Dumfries and Galloway Education Department.
7. The 'Main Report' (*Report into the pay and conditions of service of school teachers in Scotland*), Cmd 9893, HMSO. 1986.
8. See *Learning and Teaching in Scottish Secondary Schools: School Management*. HMSO 1984, and the Main Report, *op. cit.*, pp 24 ff.
9. See *Managing Progress*, Strathclyde Regional Council, 1988.
10. *Ibid*; see also Boyd, Brian, 'Letting out the reins' in *TESS*, 30 September, 1988.
11. See the reports of HM Inspectors on individual schools, issued by the SED from 1983 onwards. Since each report is reckoned to have a 'shelf-life' of only 3 or 4 years it is not appropriate to make specific references.
12. McIntyre, D., 'A School-based Development Programme' in Brown, S. and Munn, P., *The Changing Face of Education 14–16*, NFER/ Nelson. 1985.
13. *Ibid*, p. 95.
14. Simpson, M., 'School-based and centrally directed curriculum

development—the uneasy middle ground', *Scottish Educational Review*, 18(2), 1986.

15. McIntyre, *op. cit.*, p. 102.
16. Simpson, M. and Arnold, B., *The Development of Assessment in Health Studies: A Study of Curriculum Development at Standard Grade*, Mimeograph. Northern College of Education (Aberdeen Campus), 1987.
17. *Education 10–14*, pp 77, 78.
18. Kirk, G., *Teacher Education and Professional Development*, Scottish Academic Press, 1988, pp 4, 5.

CHAPTER 5

DEVELOPING THE PRIMARY CURRICULUM

1. *The 1946 curriculum*

Writing at the end of the 1960s W. Kenneth Richmond, a shrewd if rather acerbic observer of Scottish education, emphasised the 'authoritarian' character of our educational organisation: 'at no time was the pretence entertained that teachers were at liberty to teach what they pleased or how they pleased'. The master-servant relationship permeated the system. The EAs were 'firmly tied' to the apron strings of the SED in earlier days, though powers began to be delegated in the 1960s. Headteachers 'handed down' schemes of work. Faced with new ideas, Scots teachers preferred to wait and see: 'the Scots are canny—their own word for shrewdness combined with caution'. Thus the 'activity and experience' curriculum advocated by Hadow in 1931 had to wait till the 1965 Memorandum to receive official assent in Scotland.[1] This is not wholly true: the curriculum elaborated in the 1946 Advisory Council Report on Primary Education owed much to the educational scholarship and development which had underpinned the Hadow Report. Although its main emphasis lay on the improvement of subject teaching, the 1946 report also represented a significant shift towards the modern conception of a pupil-centred curriculum.

Referring to the 1872 Act's main objective as being literacy for the whole population, the 1946 report recognises the 'mere capacity to read and write' as a 'limited

objective'. More than fifty years earlier HMIs had deprecated schools' concentration on 'the beggarly elements',
as they called reading, writing and arithmetic.[2] 'Educating the whole person' was much more than a mere
slogan in Scottish schools. But the 1946 report introduced,
as formal requirements, new pedagogical emphases in
the curriculum. There was to be a shift from merely
intellectual training to the 'development of the whole
personality'. Pupils were to be considered as members of
the community, and the primary curriculum was to give
them their first training in citizenship. Pupils were to be
seen as individuals, each with a particular set of abilities
and needs; and the primary teacher was to take account
of these differences. There was to be a moving away from
whole class teaching—'hardly a satisfactory expedient for
dealing with overlarge classes'—and more individual and
group work.

A Memorandum of 1939 by HMI on nursery schooling
vividly expressed the new thinking. Nursery Schools
should aim 'to provide the right conditions for growth
and so to ensure the harmonizing of the whole personality
of the child'. Although 'teaching' is not an appropriate
term for this stage, 'the child *is* taught' by handling things,
playing, companionship—'bricks to arrange, pictures to
paint, sand to build in, water to pour, songs to sing, tables
to lay, seeds to plant, a jungle gym on which to climb,
pets to attend, questions to pose and answer, stories to
hear and tell—by such and other occupations the child's
natural energy and craving for experience are satisfied'.[3]
This classic description of an activity centred curriculum
was, of course, for non-statutory nursery schooling, but
it came to be accepted by progressive teachers of 'infants'
in the schools and the 1965 Memorandum gave this
approach the stamp of authority. During the 1950s HMIs
saw the beneficial effects of the approach in nursery
schools and encouraged teachers of P1 to adopt similar
techniques.[4]

The authors of the 1946 report could assume that all pupils would get secondary schooling of some sort, and they set out to disencumber the primary curriculum of some of the rigidity and rote learning that had 'crowded into it'. The curriculum they sought to replace was several generations old; it had been modified over time in detail but had not been 'adequately analysed by scientific methods'. Some of the subjects, or parts of them, were 'antiquated and wasteful of precious time'. There was too hard a division between subjects, and learning in that way was not natural to young children. The whole atmosphere was 'academic' rather than 'real' and the curriculum failed to appeal to the living interests of childhood. There was an emphasis on 'passivity rather than activity': the pupils were required always to 'sit still, listen, accept, and reproduce either orally or on paper'. Teachers tried to teach too much but they failed to teach the content with sufficient thoroughness.[5]

The new curriculum would be a better preparation for secondary schooling. It would teach pupils 'the use of tools' required for the later stage:

—how to speak clearly and correctly
—how to listen attentively
—how to write legibly
—how to use the fundamental rules in arithmetic
—how to make simply written statements
      —correctly spelt
      —and in properly formed sentences.

The fundamentals would be doing things, using things: physical education, handwork and speech. Physical Education (PE) would consist of exercises but also games and dancing. Handwork would give training in the use of tools and materials and take such forms as needlework for girls and 'repairs' for boys. Arithmetic would be a tool, and the pupils would go through plenty of examples of the most used processes, for example the use of fractions, money calculations, measuring and other applications which can arise in History, Geography, Drawing, Sewing, Handwork, Gardening. The working of sums would be shown more, and there would be a large amount of graded material. In Art there would be more 'observation', more discipline, more enjoyment, more visits outside. Spoken English would assume more importance, and children would learn to speak 'correctly', gracefully, fluently, building up self-confidence as a basis for learning to read. Nature Study and Geography would make use of the home area. History—the most severely criticised subject—would broaden to instil a sense of values about people and things, a greater awareness of the world, and there would be stories, discussions and active investigation of topics of interest to children. Reading and Writing should be taught as complementary activities. Grammar should not be taught at all as a formal subject in the early years, and in later years teachers should teach only the parts of speech and other 'necessary and fundamental' terms, bringing these in as part of 'Interpretation'. 'Pre-digested' textbooks should be done away with. Rote learning of poetry should be abandoned, the new emphasis being on enjoyment and training in the appreciation of quality. Written Composition should stress imagination and the expression of personality as well as practical skills. In Spelling teachers should concentrate on functional skills and words used most frequently.[6] Dictation should be given less time. In Singing, teachers should emphasise activity and enjoyment, using songs that give pleasure and interest to children. In all the relevant subjects, the curriculum should give a high priority to the traditions, language and culture of Scotland.

The Inspectorate adopted the 1946 Report's emphasis on the need for 'modern realistic methods of teaching reading and arithmetic'[7]; they urged schools to give greater importance to spoken English, and preached the need for 'clarity and fluency' without sacrificing 'national and local idiosyncracies' in speech[8]; they encouraged the building up of class libraries; they commended the use of 'project work' (which had been described in the Advisory Council's Report of 1947 on secondary education); they urged more extensive and more intelligent use of visual aids. All these 'progressive and novel ideas' came from the 1946 Report on Primary Education, which, according to the SED report to parliament for 1949, was 'undoubtedly having a stimulating influence on primary schools throughout the country'.[9] At the same time, there was a strongly conservative presence in the senior ranks of the Inspectorate, and the annual Blue Books expressed this from time to time. For many years there were references to the schools' failure to undo the ravages of war: 'the old standards have not yet been fully restored'.[10] The inspectors deplored 'a tendency to looseness of thought and expression and a prevalent feeling that one need not trouble to be accurate: anything that is near enough will do'. Pupils show less 'concentration and application than previously'—attainments in subjects requiring 'drill and revision if real proficiency is to be achieved' are 'not so good as they used to be'. There must be more emphasis on 'the necessity for hard work, a term not at all synonymous with drudgery, and less on the immediately pleasurable activities of schooling'.[11]

In October 1950 the SED published its memorandum, *The Primary School in Scotland.* This was written by a panel of HM Inspectors, and it was the curriculum elaborated there that was to be promulgated for the next fifteen years. Despite the essential conservatism of the memorandum, the Inspectors urged a number of innovative ideas in their visits to schools. They insistently encouraged group methods. They encouraged experimentation with the project method which had been described in the 1947 Secondary Report. They commended the teacher training colleges' efforts to improve teachers' knowledge and skills through courses and conferences. They strongly encouraged the efforts of the directors of education in forming panels of teachers to draw up new schemes of work. By 1953 they were admitting 'grounds for sober optimism' because teachers were 'showing an increasing awareness of modern developments'. The Blue Book for 1954 included a special report on 'Reading in the Primary School' which recommended many modern approaches such as group methods, oral work, 'look and say' word and sentence methods, study reading and the use of stories. In 1955 they reported real progress in the compiling of new schemes of work, mentioning a 'new keenness and zest' evinced by teachers in discussing the new ideals. A survey conducted that year on 'Arithmetic in the Primary School' praised a SCRE booklet on teaching arithmetic and recommended some progressive approaches such as giving pupils a 'realistic experience of number' and the use of real-life situations for problem solving.

Throughout the 1950s the inspectors kept reporting a 'disturbing feature'—the 'excessive and unnecessary preoccupation both of teachers and of pupils with promotion tests'.[12] They deprecated the 'cramming' for these tests and the consequent neglect of such subjects as History, Geography, Nature Study, in P6 and P7. In 1956 they again reported an 'undue preoccupation' with attainment tests in P6 and P7. It seemed that teachers would teach to the tests whatever anyone said so long as the tests existed; by 1958 the inspectors were pleased that 'certain areas' had abolished the common written tests for promotion to the secondary school.

The Blue Books make it clear that a national curriculum was spelled out by HM Inspectors in their series of reports on, for example, Reading, Arithmetic, and Composition, which were 'widely distributed' to schools; though their influence upon the day-to-day work done by teachers was less than was hoped, they were followed up by the inspectors in the schools.[13] The training colleges were also 'active in stimulating the interest of teachers' by holding short courses and conferences.[14] Next year the inspectors reported 'an upsurge of interest in newer methods and an increase in experiments with them', and this was greatly encouraged by the training colleges and also by reports issued by panels of teachers in, for example, Fife and East Lothian.[15]

2.   The 1965 curriculum

The Primary Memorandum, *Primary Education in Scotland*, was prepared between 1962 and 1964 by a working party which consisted of HM Inspectors, head teachers and college of education lecturers. The curriculum they constructed was hailed as 'nothing short of a revolution'[16] which gave 'official Department support to more progressive and experimental teaching techniques'.[17] As we have seen, the SED had been advocating more progressive teaching for many years. But the 1965 Memorandum did swing educational opinion markedly towards what we now call the 'child-centred curriculum'. The SED memorandum of 1950 had said that the child should be a 'willing collaborator' in his own learning; the 1965 memorandum insisted that 'the primary school child has a natural curiosity and a desire to learn which make him capable of seriously and deliberately pursuing his own education on lines of his own choice'.[18] This represented a new emphasis distinct from 'social' imperatives as the pedagogical framework of the curriculum. The 1946 memorandum had perceived the primary stage as a preparation for secondary schooling. The 1965 memorandum perceived it as a stage of development in its own right. The strong Piagetian influence on the 1965 memorandum is visible in its language of 'stages', 'growth', 'needs', 'purposes' and 'understanding'. Its fundamental principle, that each child must be allowed to progress at 'an appropriate pace, and to achieve satisfaction and success at his own level'[19] is an up-to-date restatement of the 1946 memorandum's demand for differentiated teaching in groups, but in 1965 it led to the demand for a curriculum which would cater for individual needs and interests and capacities, in which specific knowledge and skills would be less important than the 'fostering of intellectual curiosity', the 'capacity to acquire knowledge independently' and 'the urge to ask questions, and the will and ability to find the answers'.[20]

The curriculum which emerged from the 1965 memorandum can be contrasted from that of 1946 as follows:

1946–56	1965–75
Reading ⎫ Writing ⎪ Spoken English ⎬ Written Composition ⎭	Language Arts Handwriting Modern Languages
Arithmetic ⎫ Geography ⎪ History ⎬ Nature Study ⎭	Mathematics ⎫ Environmental Studies ⎬
Art and Handwork ⎫ Needlework—girls ⎬	Art and Craft Activities
Music	Music
Physical Education	Physical Education Health Education

The 1965 Memorandum reiterated the traditional Scottish belief that the school curriculum was the responsibility primarily of the headteacher, whose job it was to determine the curriculum content, the class organisation required and the allocations of time for the various activities. But there was a new emphasis on the class teacher's role. Because of the governing importance of the process of active learning, the class teacher must decide (under the head's supervision) what topics would be studied, what skills were to be acquired through given activities, and what should be the nature of the various learning activities. Henceforward there would be less concentration on developing a described curriculum than on developing the teachers' abilities to deliver a broad curricular framework in terms of actual detailed class work. The memorandum's insistence that the head's should be 'the last word' on organisation and planning and on the content of the curriculum meant that schemes of work prepared by EAs should not be allowed to dominate but should be 'useful guides' dealing only with 'broad matters of policy'.[21] It has been argued that the memorandum's recommendations were not so much 'child-centred' as 'head teacher centred'.[22] It is certainly true that the memorandum was regarded as providing sufficient general guidance on curriculum for some years to come. Writing in 1968–69, Joan Low makes this plain:

> 'Most local areas in Scotland provide their teachers with suggestions for the content and methods for various aspects of the curriculum. Individual schools are free to plan more detailed schemes but the main guidance for both content and approach is given in *Primary Education in Scotland*.'[23]

As late as 1983, the CCC's Committee on Primary Education (COPE) takes it for granted that the 1965 Memorandum should be the 'starting point' for their discussion of modern primary education. In their Position Paper of that year they say:

> 'Any broad statement on the scope and balance of the curriculum in Primary Schools in Scotland has to begin from some agreed point in time. Curriculum devel-

opment is a continuous process even if it proceeds at a different pace from one year to the next. Even if in retrospect certain historical periods seem to have produced few curricular initiatives, it is unlikely that they felt so static to those teachers living through them. Nevertheless many members of the profession will feel that the publication of "Primary Education in Scotland" in 1965 ushered in a period of unprecedented change and development. That is why the Memorandum is our obvious starting point. Although national pronouncements on the curriculum have been a regular feature for each generation since the 1930s, for many the Memorandum represented a watershed. All pronouncements from HM Inspectorate and the Consultative Committee on the Curriculum since then have been expressed in terms of pursuit of and usually failure to achieve the goals set out at that time.'[24]

By 1980 it had become a central tenet of curriculum development that change in the classrooms must be a consequence of change in the teachers. The COPE Position Paper sees participative development as 'the dominant model of curriculum development and change': 'Whereas an earlier model assumed that the deliberations of an able few could be distributed to a wider regional or national school force for implementation, it is now recognised clearly that unless teachers are involved as fully and realistically as possible in the process of change, at the stage of formulation and not merely that of implemention, little effective development is likely to take place.'[25] Despite this admirable belief the role of 'an able few' in the form of COPE at national level and working groups at regional level remained crucial. Teachers cannot be expected to think out and review the curriculum while they are actually delivering it; though teaching is a process of thinking out and reviewing, it is the learning process, rather than what is being learned, that is continuously the subject of the teacher's reflections. To examine the content of what is being taught is a process which needs to be done outside the classroom and away from constant preoccupation with pupils. Thus the curriculum development which followed the 1965 Memorandum began with a stream of applicative interpretations of its recommendations produced by groups of teachers given time for that purpose.

Over the next decade or so it was selected teachers, working with advisers and college lecturers, who constructed the new primary curriculum. Because the main work was done by professionals who could judge every proposal in the light of their experience in the classroom, it took the form of practical suggestions, specimen programmes of work, learning packages, model lessons and accounts of 'centres of interest' and successful projects. New textbooks were of course produced in great quantity, and some of these virtually dictated a curriculum in many schools. A key role was played by educational advisers who were now being appointed in considerable numbers. Especially after 1975, every regional authority appointed as many primary advisers as their circumstances allowed; by 1980 there was no EA without at least one and the majority had an advisory team. The advisers visited schools to demonstrate new ideas, present teachers with new resources and advise them on practical problems. They mounted inservice training courses. They organised seminars and conferences. Above all, they led and serviced the efforts of working groups. College of education lecturers played an important role in supporting advisers' work, conducting in-school training, being involved in curricular planning at school and regional level. As the number of students in preservice courses declined during the 1980s the colleges were allowed by the SED to assign more and more staff time to school focused inservice training and curriculum development.[26] HM Inspectors continued to encourage all these activities, and when they resumed formal school inspections they carried with them a clear set of expectations derived from the 1965 Memorandum and its developed curriculum.

3.   The COPE curriculum

The Scottish Central Committee on Primary Education and its successor, COPE, set out to create a view of curriculum which might be described as 'holistic': 'the curricular process must be ultimately individual—the outcome of the total amalgam of the learning and teaching programmes, the varying organisation of activities in the school and its classrooms, the quality of the physical environments and the nature of the human relationships that pervade all that goes on at any level in them, but only as they impinge on each individual pupil.'[27] If this means, as it seems to, that the primary school has to shape a curriculum for each pupil, and that curriculum must include all of the pupil's experience in school, the concept of *curriculum* becomes highly complex. It is clear that the extreme 'pupil-centredness' of COPE's view of curriculum puts the onus on the class teacher for designing and sustaining the 'planned experiences in which the school involves the child', and that curriculum development in this sense must be virtually synonymous with teacher development, for the central curricular aims and objectives can only be attained by the teacher working in collaboration with school colleagues. Curriculum development by external agencies becomes mainly staff development, and the object of that must be to help teachers reach new heights of professional responsibility and proficiency. In the process of defining and elaborating the components of professionality, however, the curriculum developer can suggest changes in—or propose new emphases for—the content and techniques of what is taught.

Thus the 1970s and early 1980s saw some important

developments in the curriculum proposed by the 1965 Memorandum. A more global view of the curriculum developed, the tripartite division into Language Arts, Environmental Studies and the rest being gradually replaced by a variety of models which gave different weight to the components according to the staff's pre-dilections and outlooks. Any Scottish primary school could be placed on a continuum of progressivism, as it were, the most conservative retaining subject-teaching and whole-class methods to a marked degree, and the most radical giving greater status to projects, discovery methods and individualised learning. Many schools made a crude division of time—'skills in the morning, frills in the afternoon'—betraying what COPE called 'a lack of real understanding of what was being proposed'. Throughout the 1970s a succession of reports from the SED and the CCC expressed disappointment at teachers' failure to develop the 'professional insights' which the new approaches required. An HMI report in 1971 complained that 'where class teachers have abandoned their tra-ditional methods and programmes of work they have frequently found themselves unsure of how to proceed'.[28] Increasingly in the 1970s the view was put forward that the new curriculum made demands that could only be met by 'super teachers'.

Figure 6 displays 'the range of ways in which the primary curriculum is organised', according to the Robertson Report, *Education 10–14 in Scotland*.[29] Any one of these models would have been acceptable to COPE or HMI during the early 1980s. Model 5 is clearly the most 'progressive' while Model 1 would represent the view of the primary curriculum most favoured by the Con-servative Scottish Minister of Education in 1988. The difference obviously lies in the status given to topic work and in the distinctiveness accorded to language and math-ematics as disciplines. Of course these models refer to P6 and P7 and it is taken for granted that different models

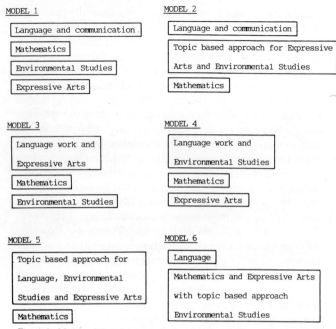

Figure 6: Models of the primary curriculum. (adapted from *Education 10–14 in Scotland,* p. 87)

might apply in different stages. The younger primary classes might well rely more on integrated topic work and the older classes on a more subject based model. What is important is that any of these models can meet the aims and objectives of the modern primary curriculum. The different emphases on particular aspects allows the school to exploit its own strengths and meet its own curricular needs. Like all the HMI and CCC documents on the primary curriculum in the period 1965 to 1988, the Robertson Report assumes that it should be pupil-centred, sustaining the pupils' 'active involvement in their own learning processes', making 'a coherent learning experience' possible, and emphasising that 'the processes and experiences of learning are as important as the content of learning'.[30] Without these essential features a curriculum cannot produce the desirable outcomes of primary education.

What we are calling the COPE curriculum differs from the 1965 curriculum in some significant respects. In Language Arts there is a new recognition of the importance of building on the child's own linguistic knowledge, and so there is a greater emphasis on speech activity, drama, language across the curriculum, language-experience methods in reading, expressive writing, imaginative literature. The 1965 Memorandum listed seven components of the Language Arts curriculum—Spoken English, Drama, Listening, Story Telling, Reading, Poetry and Written English. An important HMI report of 1981, *Learning and Teaching in P4 and P7*,[31] employed four headings, Speaking and Listening, Reading, Continuous Writing, Handwriting. COPE proposed two headings— *Language as a tool or medium* and *Language as an aesthetic discipline*—and suggested that all the required concepts and skills can be acquired by the pupils in a multitude of activities involving speaking, listening, reading, writing, self-expression, self-criticism and appreciation of creative language across the whole curriculum. COPE thus reiterated and re-emphasised the child-centred theme of the 1965 Memorandum but gave a sharper and more detailed account of the nature of language learning and teaching through their special publications on various aspects of the Language Arts curriculum.

As will be noted from Figure 6, Mathematics—which the Memorandum proposed as a component of Environmental Studies—has been assigned an important separate identity. This is because it is recognised to be one of the major disciplines necessary for a general education, but also because it underlies the specialist science and technology subjects which are so crucial to the national economy. There has also been considerable development of new curricular elements for Mathematics, such as set theory, group theory and motion geometry. Curriculum development in Mathematics has been massive in the last two decades, with large national programmes like the Nuffield Junior Mathematics Project complementing work by colleges of education staff, seconded development officers, EA advisers and working groups of teachers. There has also been very considerable development work for the production of new curricula for Environmental Studies. Almost every EA has invested heavily in setting up working groups to provide guidelines and teaching packages, in some cases relating much of the work to specific centres of interest in the locality of the schools. COPE stimulated and enriched local productivity by publishing guidance supplied by the Scottish Committee on Environmental Studies.

Another major change has been the instatement of Science as a separate discipline in many schools. In the COPE curriculum, Science is an aspect of Environmental Studies, but increasingly it is demanding and winning recognition as a subject of such importance that it requires study in depth, particularly in the older primary classes. In 1981 COPE published *Towards a Policy for Science in Scottish Primary Schools*, and HMI and other agencies have strongly encouraged schools to give a greater place to Science in the curriculum. The SED's Primary Science Development Project has been providing guidance in a series of booklets since 1985. The Robertson Report cited HMI's evidence that many primary children 'experienced little or no scientific activity in their primary career', and suggested that primary and secondary teachers should cooperate to define the concepts and skills that children need for understanding 'the process of science as a way of understanding the world'.[32] But it continued COPE's policy of integrating Science with Environmental Studies.

Another development which had occurred between the

1965 Memorandum and the COPE Position Paper of 1983 was the erection of Expressive Arts as an aspect of the curriculum to be given parity of status with Language Arts and Environmental Studies. The Memorandum did not use the term 'Expressive Arts' and devoted separate chapters to Art, Music and Physical Education, treating Drama as one of the Language Arts. In the COPE curriculum, Art, Music, Drama and Dance are regarded as the major components of Expressive Arts, and both the CCC and HMI have stressed the need for more attention—and more resources—to be given to these activities in the primary schools.

Social, Moral and Religious Education constitutes another aspect of curriculum to which the CCC has given much attention, and the relevant COPE publications are forming the basis for new development work. The Robertson Report accurately delineates the issues: though most educators would agree that 'learning processes' should exist for developing social competence and such qualities as tolerance, independence, cooperativeness and other desirable traits, it is difficult to see how teachers can provide suitable experience in a curriculum heavily laden with other content. These processes should 'permeate the curriculum' and pupils 'should be given extensive opportunities to learn to articulate their views on what is right and wrong'—but 'it is easy to dismiss such suggestions as unattainable idealism'.[33] The most up-to-date term in use to describe such aspects of the curriculum is Values Education: that is, the study of the basic values that contribute to the growth of good citizenship. Distinct from Religious Education—which of course is also an essential element of the curriculum—Values Education deals with the pupil as an individual in relation to the family, the peer group, the community and society at large; it seeks to involve the pupils in discussions, projects and other experiences designed to help them contemplate, and where appropriate make use of in their own lives, the attitudes and beliefs which underlie desirable human behaviour. The importance of this aspect of the primary school curriculum has been recognised in the acceptance by the SED and the SCCC of a grant from the Gordon Cook Foundation for the setting up of a Values Education centre and programme.

There are other claims for a place in the modern primary school curriculum. Many schools include Outdoor Education in the form of skiing, hill walking, sailing and other pursuits. Some EAs have required schools to adapt a positive learning programme to promote the principles of multi-cultural education. Many schools have teaching programmes designed to further their pupils' awareness of health and problems such as drugs, AIDS, tobacco and alcohol abuse. Some schools have specially designed programmes related to money management, school-industry relations, international affairs and peace studies. An increasingly important component of Environmental Studies, the study of issues related to the conservation of our natural heritage, is being developed in many schools. There is now a renewed interest in the teaching of a foreign language (mainly French) or 'language awareness' which is teaching about languages designed to prepare pupils for the study of any foreign language.

4. *Abatement of the primary curriculum*

In October 1988 the Secretary of State announced the government's intention to press ahead with a 'review of the balance of the primary curriculum'. The SCCC have been invited to produce 'clearer and more structured advice' on the balance of the curriculum and to 'establish guidelines setting out for each aspect of the curriculum the aims of study, the content to be covered and the objectives to be achieved'. Priority must be given to 'English' and Mathematics—'but in the interests of preserving curricular balance it will be important that all areas of the curriculum are reviewed and new guidelines developed as soon as possible'. Parallel guidelines are to be produced for parents. The revised curriculum will be monitored by different means: by means of inspection by HMI, by means of reports by headteachers to school boards, and by means of supervision by the EA. Standardised tests will be administered to all pupils in P4 and P7, and the testing procedures will also be monitored. The Secretary of State's aim in all this is 'to give greater direction and purpose to Scottish education and better to equip our children for the challenges of the 21st century'.[34]

It is easy to infer the educational effects aimed at in these proposals. In the first place there is to be a marked shift of responsibility for curriculum away from the teachers towards the central authorities. The 'balance' of the curriculum—that is, the status given to various aspects in terms of assigned time and attention—is to be defined by the SCCC instead of by the school, as has been the policy which emerged from the 1965 Memorandum and the work of the CCC. The teachers will no longer be able to exercise professional judgement about the content of teaching programmes because, although the guidelines are to be advisory, the inspectors and parents will be empowered to check on the teachers' use of them. And because the SCCC will specify the aims of study and the content to be covered for every aspect of the curriculum there is bound to be a shift away from the principle that what is done in the classroom should be derived from the interests of the pupils 'there and then'. For the same reason there will be a shift away from the principle that each pupil should progress at his or her own pace: individualised learning is not compatible with a prescribed coverage of content.

Secondly, the balance of the curriculum is being deliberately disturbed by assigning a high priority to language and number work. The tell-tale specification of 'English' instead of 'Language Arts' proclaims a calculated rejection of the central principle of the 1965 and COPE curricula, that the language skills should be developed mainly through interdisciplinary activities. Coupled with the imposition of standardised tests, this reversion to a primitive conception of language learning must inevitably discourage the use of the topic approach and drive teachers towards 'teaching to the test', a practice deplored in the government's reports throughout the 1950s. Similarly, standardised testing in Mathematics will discourage the teaching in real-life contexts which has characterised the curriculum in recent years; moreover, it is implied in the Secretary of State's statement of intent that it will be mainly Arithmetic that is tested—the evidence lies in his use of such terms as 'numeracy' and 'key elements'—although the SED's AAP tests do assess other aspects of Mathematics.[35]

These proposals represent a rejection of the curriculum which has been painstakingly developed over the last quarter century, and an attempt to impel schools towards the simplistic subject-centred curriculum of the pre-1965 era. The developed modern curriculum is complex and delicate, depending for its educational impact on the high professionality of the teachers. It has been asseverated over many years that it is too complex, too sensitive, too teacher-dependent; and certainly many teachers find it hard to develop the professional judgement required to ascertain, for each pupil at any given moment, what are the concepts being assimilated and what are the skills being learned from a particular activity.[36] By and large, however, the COPE curriculum *is* being successfully delivered in the majority of our classrooms, according to the reports of HMI. To revert clumsily to an outdated and educationally invalid curriculum is bound to be destructive to teachers and harmful to pupils. It is to some degree reassuring, however, that the Secretary of

State's press release of October 1988 exhibits some awareness of these dangers. He acknowledges the 'fears'
expressed by many respondents to his proposals that they
would cause a 'reduction in teachers' scope to organise
classroom activities', and he promises that 'all areas
of the curriculum' will be reviewed 'in the interests of
preserving curricular balance'. He admits that many
respondents expressed the conviction that 'tests might
distort the curriculum by forcing or encouraging teachers
to teach to the test' and he undertakes that 'particular
attention' will be given in the preparation of guidelines
to this problem. It is to be hoped that the professional
officers responsible for implementing the government's
political purposes will be able to salvage a significant
measure of the integrity of the modern primary curriculum.

REFERENCES

1. Richmond, W. Kenneth, *The School Curriculum*, Methuen. 1971. pp 133 ff.
2. See Kerr, John, *Memories Grave and Gay*, Blackwood, 1903, and Gatherer, W. A., 'Reading and the Scottish Tradition' in Anderson, C., ed., *Reading: the ABC and Beyond*. Macmillan. 1988.
3. Quoted in *Primary Education*. HMSO. 1946.
4. HM Inspectors' work in school was referred to in most of the Blue Books for 1950–1960.
5. *Education in Scotland in 1946* (Blue Book). HMSO. 1947, p. 19.
6. The Report calls for more research on the teaching of spelling. This was undertaken by SCRE in the 1950s.
7. *Education in Scotland in 1949*. HMSO. 1950, p. 17.
8. *Ibid.*
9. *Ibid.*
10. *Education in Scotland in 1951*. HMSO. 1952.
11. *Education in Scotland in 1950*. HMSO. 1951, p. 13.
12. *Education in Scotland in 1954*. HMSO. 1955, p. 21.
13. *Education in Scotland in 1957*. HMSO. 1958, p. 11.
14. *Ibid.*

15. *Education in Scotland in 1958*. HMSO. 1959. p. 11.
16. See Osborne, G. S., *Scottish and English Schools*, University of Pittsburg. 1966.
17. Hunter, S. L., *The Scottish Educational System*. Pergamon. 1972.
18. *Primary Education in Scotland*. HMSO. 1965, p. 12.
19. *Ibid*, p. 4.
20. *Ibid*, p. 18.
21. *Ibid*, p. 39.
22. McEnroe, F. J., 'Freudianism, Bureaucracy and Scottish Primary Education' in *Scottish Culture and Scottish Education*, ed. Humes, W. M. and Paterson, H. M. John Donald. 1983.
23. Low, J., 'Primary Schools', in Nisbet, J. and Kirk, Gordon, eds., *Scottish Education Looks Ahead*. Chambers. 1969, p. 14.
24. *Primary Education in the Eighties*. CCC. 1983, p. 7.
25. *Ibid*, p. 7.
26. See Kirk, Gordon, *Teacher Education and Professional Development*. Scottish Academic Press. 1988.
27. *Primary Education in the Eighties*. CCC. 1983, p. 9.
28. *Primary Education: Organisation for Development*. HMSO. 1971.
29. Adapted from *Education 10–14 in Scotland*. CCC. 1986, p. 87.
30. *Ibid*, p. 86.
31. *Learning and Teaching in P4 and P7*. HMSO. 1981.
32. *Education 10–14 in Scotland*. CCC. 1986, p. 52.
33. *Ibid*, pp 38–9.
34. Scottish Office Press Release, 3 October 1988.
35. See *Achievement of Scottish School Children in Mathematics*. Assessment of Achievement Programme. SED. 1988.
36. For a useful discussion of these issues see Skinner, D., 'Ever increasing circles' in *TESS*, 20 May 1988.

CHAPTER 6

DEVELOPING THE SECONDARY CURRICULUM

1. *The 1947 curriculum*

The curriculum constructed by the Advisory Council of 1947 represented a considerable advance towards the modern secondary curriculum: their insistence that 'the good school is to be assessed not by any tale of examination successes, however impressive, but by the extent to which it has filled the years of youth with security, graciousness and ordered freedom'[1] reflects a view strongly held today. Hence they set out to design a curriculum from first principles, abjuring the traditional habit of merely adding to the 'array of subjects' as new interests emerge. They were determined not to assume that every subject in the traditional curriculum was sacrosanct and not to be considered for exclusion. 'Present relevance' rather than 'past prestige' was to be the main criterion.

The Advisory Council proposed a 'core and periphery' curriculum model. The core they favoured comprised Physical Education, Handicrafts, the Arts and Religious Education with the 'intellectual studies', Spoken and Written English, Number and Spatial Relationships, General Science and Social Studies. These were studies to be followed by all secondary pupils. The 'peripheral' studies, to be undertaken by the abler minority, were Mathematics (the 'more exacting parts'), Modern Languages, Classics and 'certain vocational studies' such as Commercial Subjects.[2] They were advocating an 'omni-

bus' secondary school which all pupils in a neigh-
bourhood would attend, and this was a curriculum clearly
designed for a comprehensive school catering for the
whole range of ability. Along with their proposals for the
content of the curriculum they recommended various
teaching approaches—such as the Dalton Plan, project
methods, centres of interest—which later became
received wisdom. They also recommended features of
school curricular organisation which have still not
become standard practice in Scottish schools. For
example, they came near to proposing a 'negotiated curriculum' when they suggested that at the beginning of
each term the pupils should be given 'some indication' of
the range of work to come, and that 'graphical or other
devices' should be used to show to what extent the programme is being fulfilled'.[3] They suggested that schools
should experiment with activity afternoons, hobby
periods and so on (a scheme later proposed in the CCC's
Ruthven Report in 1967 but never widely adopted in
Scotland). They urged that extra-curricular activities
such as debate and dramatic work should be included in
the formal curriculum. They advocated a greater use
of visits and excursions to supplement school studies.
Significantly, they recommended efforts to 'socialise' the
teaching: by using discussions and various forms of pupil
interaction in large measure to 'transfer the control of
class-activity from the teacher to the pupils themselves';
and 'by substituting for competition, individual rivalry,
and the familiar machinery of marks and merit lists' to
create 'a truly cooperative spirit' where 'youngsters are
not merely allowed but encouraged to help one another'.[4]

Although the major recommendations of the Advisory
Council in relation to national examinations were rejected
by the Secretary of State, the SED reported in 1949 that
he was 'in general agreement' with most of the Report's
'numerous recommendations', and promised a series of
circulars and memoranda dealing with the organisation

and curriculum of the secondary school'.[5] Consequently there were issued memoranda on Art, Commercial Subjects, Classics, Science, History, Geography, Technical Subjects and Modern Languages (in 1951); Homecraft, Rural Subjects, Music and English (in 1952). These were prepared by panels of inspectors and written in the drier official style of SED papers, but by and large they echoed most of the Advisory Council pleas for more relevance and more practical interest in the subject curricula. Since no government of the time had any idea of moving towards the Advisory Council's concept of an 'omnibus' school, the subject syllabuses continued to be designed with the Leaving Certificate requirements in mind, the backwash effects of the external examination determining the whole of the curriculum for the secondary schools. It was for the Junior Secondary schools, which catered for the less academic and less affluent majority of pupils in the cities and larger burghs, that the Advisory Council's more liberal and progressive curricular policies were promulgated by the inspectors.

The SED officials were well aware that there were 'formidable problems in devising curricula to suit the varied aptitudes and interests' of Junior Secondary pupils. The inspectors tried hard to introduce new ideas, but the curriculum in these schools stubbornly remained watered down versions of the Secondary school curriculum. But here and there a more pupil-centred programme emerged: some schools based much of their work on projects and topics; some used the environment creatively; some introduced novel approaches such as drama, library periods and school visits to factories and farms; some introduced pottery, weaving, puppetry; some developed new curricula for home-making, housewifery, farm management.[6]

The inspectors reported that newly appointed supervisors for Art had 'been able to assist and inspire teachers'; gradually, throughout the 1950s, more and more advisory teachers were appointed mainly for Art, Music, Technical Education and Homecraft. They made little impact on the Leaving Certificate syllabuses but they greatly improved the teaching of their subjects in the schools by providing more and better equipment and encouraging teachers to study new approaches. They were particularly influential in the Junior Secondary schools, and contributed valuably to the development of new curricular ideas which came to fruition in the comprehensive schools in the 1970s. These EA advisers turned to the teacher training colleges for help in mounting courses, and by the early 1960s there had developed a new partnership for curriculum development among inspectors, advisers and college lecturers.

2.   Developing subject curricula

During the 1950s the publication of an SED memorandum on a subject would be followed by conferences of teachers, lecturers and inspectors to discuss the subject's aims, content and methods of instruction. At this time, as we have seen, the inspectors were beginning to adopt decisive leadership roles. Brunton deliberately sought to appoint specialists who could bring new knowledge and insights into the Inspectorate, and encouraged them to devote a significant proportion of their time to developing new ideas and approaches. As Brunton put it many years later, the recommendations of the working party on the curriculum of the senior secondary school (which proposed the introduction of a new fourth-year examination in 1959) 'removed the rigidities from the curriculum, gave it a new fluidity and flexibility, and gave to headmasters and teachers a new freedom to plan courses suited to the needs of their pupils and to the teaching of their subjects'. For Brunton, the great need was to 'modernise the curriculum'.[7] He was himself a restless, innovative thinker, and he actively stimulated the younger inspectors to put their ideas down on paper and 'take them round the schools, the universities and colleges', to organise conferences and to persuade directors and headteachers to support experimental projects in schools.

In this manner new syllabuses were introduced in the early 1960s in Science, Mathematics and Modern Studies. Donald McGill, a teacher in Glasgow Academy, was appointed HMI in 1959 at the unusually late age of 49 for the express purpose of developing Physics; he was soon leading a group of teachers in pilot studies and in 1962 a new (alternative) syllabus in Physics was published.[8] For Mathematics a new syllabus was produced in 1963 by a committee of teachers, lecturers and inspectors. For Modern Studies, a new subject combining elements of History, Geography and Economics, all related to the contemporary world, new syllabuses were produced from 1962 onwards; again the main impetus came from an inspector, W. K. Ferguson, working closely with selected colleagues from schools, colleges and universities. English teachers were startled when inspectors began to decry old fashioned grammar and mechanical exercises and talk about new content and approaches deriving from the science of linguistics. Brunton, himself a modern linguist, arranged for a young HMI to liaise with university scholars in Scotland and in England, write memoranda on the new ideas, and persuade teachers of English and college lecturers to come together and devise entirely new schemes of language study.[9] By the time the Central Committee on English was set up in 1966 many English specialists were already excited about 'the new English' and eager to work for changes in the curriculum.

The period between 1965 and 1980 saw an enormous flowering of subject curricula in Scotland. The CCC and its Central Committees produced a large number of papers devoted to the separate disciplines, each discussing the aims and objectives of the subject, outlining the desirable content and describing the most effective methods of teaching. Whole new curricula were thus published for English, Mathematics, Physical Education, Science, the Social Subjects, Modern Languages, Religious Education, Home Economics, Technical Education, Art, Music, Business Studies, Latin and Classical Studies, Drama; new subjects and courses were introduced such as Integrated Science, Economics, Craft and Design, Computing, Social Education. In all of the established subjects taught in secondary schools there was what amounted to a revolution: new content, new approaches, new resources were advocated, experimented with and in varying degrees adopted as normal components of the school curriculum.[10] Because the Central Committees were virtually autonomous until the CCC set up COSE in 1976, there was little or no attempt to study the secondary curriculum as a whole. In accordance with the Scottish tradition, each school was left to compile its own curriculum without central guidance as to its purposes, aims or operational character. Despite the huge amount of guidance made available for the individual subject departments there was little advice for heads and their senior colleagues as to how the different subjects were to be knit together to form a coherent educational experience for the pupils.

There was, certainly, much unease about the proliferation of demands being made upon the curriculum. As the subject curricula developed they encouraged teachers to increase the content—or the time taken to cover it—and to want more opportunities to pursue teaching activities. Mixed ability grouping in S1 and S2 often led teachers to feel anxious about having too little time to do a topic justice. Guidance and Social Education had to be slotted into the curriculum at the expense of some other subjects. The development of Outdoor Education and the greater use of the environment took pupils away for periods of time which had to be docked off the formal curriculum timetable. Above all, new curricular elements were beginning to need formal recognition: for example, Computing, Drama, Careers Education, link courses in Further Education colleges. Novel methods of timetabling were devised, but the main problem remained. The secondary curriculum was grossly overcrowded.

3.   The search for balance

In 1976 an important document was published by the CCC: Curriculum Paper 15, *The Social Subjects in Secondary Schools*.[11] This contained the first official discussion of the question of balance in the curriculum in Scottish secondary schools—a question that had been dealt with eleven years earlier in respect of the primary curriculum. The Scottish Central Committee on Social Subjects provided thoughtful accounts of the social and educational purposes of their subjects and discussed these in the light of modern philosophical theories of curriculum developed by Phenix and Hirst; they also related their subjects to the educational psychology of learning developed by Piaget and Bruner. They posed the questions: 'what are the essential elements of a balanced curriculum? how far is balance a matter of content coverage as distinct from mental process? how far can balance be reconciled with specialisation?'[12] The Commitee could not deal at length with these questions (which were being pondered at the time by the Munn Committee) but they considered the problem of balance *within* the Social Subjects; and this led them to examine the question of 'how far curricular structure should be discipline-based and how far based on integrated studies'. The Committee came down in favour of the discipline-centred curriculum; but their argument embraced the possibility of achieving the integration of various elements of disciplines in the form of specially designed courses. They posited six approaches to the provision of programmes of learning:

1. Pure subject teaching without any deliberate attempt to use contributions from other disciplines.
2. Outward-looking subject-teaching seeking links with other subjects.
3. Outward-looking subject-teaching with cooperation between different subject departments.
4. Course based on linked subject units, drawing on more than one discipline.
5. Single, fused or synthesised course drawing from more than one discipline with team teaching.
6. Single, fused or synthesised course taught by a single teacher.

Thus they emphasised the potential of the traditional discipline-based curriculum for achieving greater balance by means of multidisciplinary courses.

The Munn Committee, set up by the CCC in 1975 to review the curriculum of the third and fourth years of secondary education, were specifically charged with the task of considering how the curriculum can be structured to provide 'a balanced education'.[13] They found the concept of balance 'elusive'. Nonetheless they designed a curriculum for S3 and S4, the period of study leading to the old Ordinary Grade and the new Standard Grade, and founded their decisions on a clearly delineated specification of what they meant by balance. They posited eight 'modes of activity or fields of study' which should yield a 'balanced education' to all pupils; and from this matrix they extrapolated a detailed curriculum framework.[14] The details of this framework were debated and worked over for several years by the CCC and others; some features were added and some modified; and it was not until the CCC produced its definitive *Curriculum Design for the Secondary Stages* in 1987 that it was possible to perceive and evaluate a whole new curriculum which could claim to have met the requirements for a balanced education remitted to the Munn Committee ten years before.

4. Development programmes 1977–1987

This was a period of unprecedented activity in curriculum development in Scotland. More than two dozen reports were issued at national level, most of them resulting in substantial development programmes and some of them resulting in fundamental changes in teachers' perceptions of their role in developing the curriculum. The EAs were now taking a more active interest in curriculum and staff development, and their many different working groups were producing a mass of curricular materials. In schools new mechanisms for reviewing, evaluating and developing curriculum were becoming better established and more effective. Even a couple of years of bitter industrial conflict between teachers and government failed to stem the tide of productivity, though the unions unhappily attacked curriculum development by attempting to impose a boycott on it.

The most conspicuous development project was the SED's 'Munn and Dunning Development Programme' (MDDP) launched in 1980 after the Secretary of State had accepted modified versions of the Munn Report on curriculum and the Dunning Report on assessment. There was no question about the methodology to be adopted for the design, piloting and promulgation of the new S3–4 curriculum during the 1980s. A Development Unit was set up in the SED, and the administrators and inspectors who manned it rigorously controlled the management of funds, staffing and dissemination of materials. Joint Working Parties (JWP) representing the SED, the CCC and the SEB were set up to produce guidelines and syllabuses for every subject, in most cases at three levels of academic difficulty, Credit, General and Foundation. Watered down versions of the Dunning Report's recommendations about in-school teacher

assessment were worked out and for most of the syllabuses, but particularly for those at Foundation Level, a
measure of course work and teacher assessment was built
in. The Munn Report's grudging concession of the value
of interdisciplinary studies was accepted to the extent
that some courses were designed to teach Contemporary
Social Studies, Health Studies and Social and Vocational
Skills, all subjects that had been given priority by politicians. Overriding priority was assigned by the government to English, Mathematics and Science. The SED's
domination of the whole programme was pronounced.

Nevertheless the programme produced many excellent
results. A wide ranging research and development policy
gave impetus to a number of important investigations
and experiments, especially in respect of techniques for
curriculum development and assessment involving
schools and their teachers. Every JWP made extensive
use of the documentation produced over the years by
HMI and the CCC and its Central Committees, so that
almost all the new subject curricula were progressive and
to some extent pupil-centred, with modern techniques of
teaching and assessment. The production of the new
subject curricula was phased over a period of some six
years: in the event the completion of the whole programme will have taken more than a decade.

Another important governmental programme was
launched in 1983 by the publication of an 'Action Plan'
for developing a new curriculum for the tertiary stage,
specifically for the 16–18 year-olds not proceeding to
higher education.[15] This was a bold and radical plan to
reform the whole provision of Further Education courses,
and it led swiftly to the establishment of a new Scottish
Vocational Education Council (SCOTVEC) with a com-
pletely new system of curriculum delivery, assessment
and certification. SCOTVEC and the National Certificate are now rightly famed throughout the world.[16].
In curricular terms, the importance of this programme

can hardly be exaggerated. Every course has been analysed and redesigned in the form of 40-hour modules.
Each module is described in terms of its aims, pedagogical
objectives and content. For each module, guidance has
been elaborated on its pedagogical purpose, the learning
outcomes expected, the content to be covered, the kinds
of assessment suggested, and the module's relationship
with preceding and subsequent modules. All this information is provided in *module descriptors*, many hundreds
of which are issued periodically by SCOTVEC. The
advantages of this new curriculum design are numerous:
it offers much greater scope to curriculum developers by
enabling them to add, delete or integrate units of study
in a course; it allows more curricular balance because a
variety of studies can more easily be linked; it facilitates
the construction of individual curricula, since any student
can virtually design a personal curriculum by selecting
modules; it allows students more choice; above all, it
makes a course more *visible* in that it is easier to see what
it consists of and what it requires of the student and the
teacher.

The CCC had been debating the issue of short courses
for some years before the initiation of the Action Plan.
Short free-standing courses seemed to offer solutions to a
number of curricular problems. They would allow a much
greater diversity of studies in the secondary curriculum,
thus catering for the increasingly numerous demands
from pressure groups to include more courses. They
would allow schools to cater more efficiently for the
personal interests of pupils. They would provide more
flexibility to curriculum developers because a short course
can easily be added, amended or replaced in a two-year
course (or 'cluster', the term used to denote a grouping
of short courses). The design and coordination of course
clusters would encourage cooperation among teachers of
different subjects. Short courses were particularly attractive for teachers engaged in Guidance activities, and

teachers of such subjects as Religious Education and Physical Education whose areas of desirable teaching content are wide and diverse. Above all, short courses would offer a greater range of educational experience to pupils, thus leading to the Munn Committee's ideal of a broad and balanced curriculum for all.[17] The CCC's Short Course Programme, started in 1981, stimulated the design of many short courses in schools on such topics as Theatre Arts, Traffic Education, Fire Education, Graphics, Photography, Kitchen Gardening and many others. By the time the modular curriculum came to be widely known many schools were interested in developing short courses, and their efforts were easily and conveniently adapted to join with the new plan. TVEI schemes stimulated this movement. A large number of schools now offer SCOTVEC modular courses to their 14 to 16 year-olds, and it has become obvious that the Higher Grade courses leading to the Scottish Certificate of Education in S5 or S6 could readily be modularised. Indeed, as the Robertson Report on *Education 10–14* made clear, there are reasons to believe that 'a predominantly modular structure may become the norm in secondary schools'.[18] In the meantime, however, the SED is averse to a full-scale transition to a modular curriculum. In its Circular on the 'Use of Nationally Certified Short Courses in Schools' the Department expresses the belief that short courses 'can fulfil a valuable function in a number of different contexts, in particular by adding balance, variety and flexibility to the curriculum'; but it is proposed that short courses should merely supplement two-year courses. The modular construction of short courses, however, is endorsed, and it is suggested that they should be assessed internally and on the basis of outcomes achieved in the manner adopted for all SCOT-VEC modules. Thus a significant step has been taken towards the modularisation of the S3–S4 curriculum.[19]

The CCC's EISP and the subsequent work of SEIC

strongly influenced the secondary curriculum, particularly less academic courses for the 14+ age group. The PPC and SEIC have issued many subject-oriented reports, devised new courses, arranged for 'curricular inserts' in examination syllabuses, and encouraged the extension of Industrial Studies, work experience and the appointment of Education Industry Liaison Officers (EILOs). The new government-sponsored drive for Enterprise Education (the promotion of self-confidence, entrepreneurial ability and interest in business) and the many industry-related courses in TVEI all owe their origins to EISP. A new awareness and concern for the needs of industry and commerce is now well established in schools; at the same time, the PPC's concern to preserve the general cultural value of the curriculum has been supported widely, so that the government's enthusiasm for vocational training has not been allowed to distort the curriculum.

5. Curriculum design for the secondary stages

In 1987 the CCC issued 'Guidelines for Headteachers' on the secondary school curriculum. This was the culmination of the CCC's efforts over a decade to develop a rationale which would 'ensure coherence, continuity, articulation and progression in the curriculum'.[20] The Guidelines offer curriculum descriptions based on the Munn Report and various other documents issued by the SED or the CCC. They presuppose a National Curricular Framework, as described in HMI reports and CCC papers, and they take it for granted that it is the function of EAs to assist schools to adapt national guidance to local circumstances: 'from the national curricular framework and within authority policy, each school, college or consortium will select and develop courses and modules'.[21] They do not consider the situation which might arise if EA policy were to be at odds with SED or

CCC policies. They accept, however, that 'to a limited extent at S1/S2, and to an increasing degree from S3 to S6' schools are free to select programmes appropriate to the needs and aspirations of each pupil.

The CCC repeat the three 'claims' on the secondary curriculum posited by the Munn Committee: the demands of knowledge, which derive from the distinctive skills, concepts, logical structure and methodology of a discipline or subject; the psychological needs of the pupil; and the requirements of society. From these 'claims' they derive a set of 'general curricular aims' as these were set out by the Munn Committee: the development of knowledge and understanding; the development of cognitive, interpersonal and psychomotor skills; the affective development of pupils in behavioural attitudes; and preparation for life and development of social competence. They see three stages in secondary schooling: at S1/2 emphasis should be laid upon the development of skills, knowledge and self-understanding; at S3/4 there must be emphasis on the application of knowledge and skills in a range of specialised courses; and at S5/6 the emphasis moves to vocationally-oriented, specialised and individualised courses in preparation for working life or higher education.

The Guidelines propose three distinct kinds of curriculum components: *elements* which should permeate the curriculum, *modes of activity* necessary to achieve breadth and balance in the curriculum, and *activities* which can be regarded as optional. Permeating elements are of two kinds: *process skills* such as language and numeracy competencies, learning strategies and problem solving; and *aspects of personal and social development* such as health, responsibility, understanding and tolerance, care of the environment and critical appreciation of the media. This ingenious analysis of curriculum content allows the inclusion in the rationale of all the studies, activities and experiences proposed in recent times for inclusion in the secondary curriculum. 'Permeation' means including in all courses some learnings or experiences designed to develop in pupils the appropriate skills or attitudes; but this goal can be achieved also through 'syllabus inserts' or specialised short courses or modules. Thus the Guidelines provide a convenient method for the promotion of 'language across the curriculum', 'Mathematics for all', 'Social Education' and other current curricular demands.

From the Munn and Robertson Committees the CCC derived the notion of 'modes of activity' or 'aspects of experience', and the Guidelines recommend that the curriculum for S1 to S4 should contain eight distinct modes of study and activity: Language and Communication, Mathematical Studies and Applications, Scientific Studies and Applications, Creative and Aesthetic Activities, Technological Activities and Applications, Social and Environmental Studies, Religious and Moral Education and Physical Education. A whole curriculum of subject courses can be designed on this framework; but alternatively the modes can be apportioned among a mixed diet of courses of differing length and content. 'Balance and breadth' can be obtained by ensuring that every pupil benefits from all the modes.

The CCC, however, recognise that different values are attached to the various modes, and they recommend a range of time allocations. For example, they suggest for S1/2 that over two years the class time given to Language and Communication should average 22%, for Mathematical Studies 12%, for Religious and Moral Education 5%, for PE 7% and for all other modes 10% each; this leaves 14% of class time available for guidance, remediation or additional study in one of the modes. For S3/4 they recommend a core curriculum in which each mode is allocated a minimum and maximum time percentage, and their distribution leaves 35% of the time for an 'elective' area, to be used for additional studies within the eight modes or additional short courses made available by the school. Since the initiation of the Munn and Dunning Programme the government has insisted that English, Mathematics and Science should form a compulsory 'inner core' for S3/4, so the CCC Guidelines allocate 35% of class time to these subjects.

Despite the liberalising effect of the notion of 'permeating elements', however, the curriculum proposed by the CCC is like that proposed by the Munn Committee, essentially the old orthodox subject-based curriculum of Scottish educational tradition. For S1/2, for example, there is to be a Core Area comprising English and a Foreign Language, Mathematics, Science, Art, Music and Drama, Technical Education, Home Economics, Social Subjects, Religious, Moral and Social Education and Physical Education; and there is a list of examples of activities under the label 'Enrichment', such as additional languages, Media Studies, Computer Applications, Money Management, Electronics, Design, 'Mini-Enterprises', Classical Studies, 'Caring', Health Studies—all assigned theoretically to one of the eight modes. The CCC have not yet discussed alternative curricular patterns nor recommended experimentation with school-designed curricula.

Nevertheless, the Guidelines offer headteachers a comprehensive matrix for their curricular plans. A timetable based upon these suggestions ought certainly to provide a broad and balanced education to all the pupils. The Guidelines do not usurp the school managers' responsibility for allocating pupils to courses, and courses to the curriculum. Nor do they specify what should be the salient characteristics of the individual curricula designed for pupils. So long as the Guidelines are mere guidelines, they will surely be accepted as excellent aids to curriculum developers at all levels in the system. But it is plain that even in this document there are intimations of central control which have already perturbed headteachers: there is a prescribed core curriculum. The government has gone further, however, in its statement of intentions towards the curriculum: it proposes to exert control over the delivery of the curriculum by means of formal inspection and compulsory reports by heads to School Boards. Thus the national curricular framework which the CCC has provided might well become a National Curriculum prescribed by the state. Already a Circular on the provision of languages other than English seems bound to force schools to include Modern Languages in the core area for S3/4. It remains to be seen whether the time-honoured autonomy of schools in curriculum provision will give way altogether to the kind of centralist prescription the present generation of educators had forgotten ever existed.

6. *The new authoritarianism*

A new kind of centralist prescription is now a present reality in Scotland. The inauguration of the S Grade and Action Plan development programmes marked an important change in the style of educational government in Scotland. Scottish teachers have long been familiar with authoritarian curriculum prescriptions: they have been characterised as docile, willing to follow a given lead, accepting innovations 'dumped on the school's doorstep without much in the way of prior notice or by-your-leave'.[22] But in the past the 'authorities' constituted EAs and various consultative bodies as well as the SED. In the 1980s, the SED began to assert its predominance over all other sources of authority in an unprecedented way.

There was now open reference to the '*Government's* Development programme'. Both for the S Grade developments and the institution of the National Certificate, the SED set up mechanisms for what they called 'a structured programme of implementation'.[23] A group of SED officers not only controlled the management and resources but provided 'clear remits' to all the 'development teams' they set up. Although they were recruited from colleges of education and schools, the developers were made firmly responsible to inspectors who were in turn responsible to administrators acting as agents of the Minister. The guidelines and syllabuses produced by innumerable working parties were all carefully scrutinised in the Department and issued only after approval had been gained at a high level. In the new parlance of business management training, the 'cascade' model of dissemination was employed: that is to say, 'guidelines' and specifications were prepared by a 'cadre of trainers' and passed on to group leaders and thence to the workforce.

The movement towards governmental control of the curriculum, which was manifested throughout Britain, was deeply resented: such terms as 'interference' and 'totalitarian' were levelled at Ministers.[24] In Scotland the excessive demands made of teachers by government officers and their seconded assistants sharpened the teachers' resentment of highhanded political responses to salary claims, and in the course of a long industrial dispute they seriously undermined the government's plans by boycotting both curriculum and staff development activities. Despite the fact that the guidelines and syllabuses for Standard Grade were produced with the aid of a large number of expert teachers, and piloted and evaluated extensively in schools, they carried an inevitable taint of centralist authoritarianism. They went far to 'effect a reconciliation', writes Kirk, 'between what have hitherto tended to be regarded as irreconcilable demands: the need for central control of the curriculum and the need for school-based curriculum development'.[25] But they introduced a new imperious style of curriculum development which has antagonised the majority of educators.

During 1987 and 1988 the new Minister of Education, Michael Forsyth, took the movement towards a totalitarian curriculum a step further by identifying himself publicly with the unpopular 'reforms'. He engaged in a polemical defence of policies which came increasingly under critical fire from the teaching profession, with the result that Scottish education has become politicised as it has never been before. The notion of 'mandatory guidelines' was invented to signify the government's determination to exert control over the processes of education, including the curriculum and assessment procedures. Innovations which, in the past, would have been suggested to advisory bodies, worked out by study groups and subjected to widespread consultation have recently been promulgated in the form of terse circulars and announced abruptly in the course of political speeches or interviews. The Scottish educational system now faces many difficulties, not the least of which is the threat of a new authoritarianism which could well destroy much of the progress we have made over the last quarter century.

REFERENCES

1. *Secondary Education*, HMSO. 1947, p. 10.
2. *Ibid.* pp. 19 ff.
3. *Ibid.* p. 27.
4. *Ibid.* p. 27.
5. *Education in Scotland in 1948*, HMSO. 1949.
6. *Education in Scotland in 1949*, HMSO. 1950. p. 19.
7. McPherson and Raab, *op. cit.*, p. 89.
8. Bone, T. R., *op. cit.*, p. 231.
9. Personal recollection: the HMI in question was the present writer.
10. For accounts of new subject curricula in the 1980s see *Educating for Tomorrow*, ed. Gatherer, W. A. and Wallace B., Holmes McDougall. 1984.
11. Published by HMSO in 1976.
12. *Ibid.*, p. 11.
13. *The Structure of the Curriculum in the Third and Fourth Years of the Scottish Secondary School*. HMSO. 1977. (The Munn Report).

14. For an important discussion of the Munn Committee's work, see Kirk, G., *Curriculum and Assessment in the Scottish Secondary School: A Study of the Munn and Dunning Reports*. Ward Lock Educational. 1982. For an account of how schools set about implementing the Munn Report, see O'Malley, T. J., in *Educating for Tomorrow*, ed. Gatherer, W. A. and Wallace, B., Holmes McDougall. 1984.

15. *16–18s in Scotland: An Action Plan*. SED. 1983.

16. For information about National Certificate see the publications of SCOTVEC, Hanover House, Glasgow. For a critical discussion of the curricular provision see Weir, A. D., *Education and Vocation 14–18*. Scottish Academic Press. 1988.

17. See *Short Courses: the Final Evaluation Report on the CCC's Short-Course Programme 1981–83*. CCC. 1984.

18. *Education 10–14 in Scotland*. CCC. 1986, p. 111.

19. Circular No. 1157, *Use of Nationally Certified Short Courses in Schools*, July 1987.

20. *Curriculum Design for the Secondary Stages*. CCC. 1987, p. 1.

21. *Ibid.*, p. 3.

22. Richmond, W. Kenneth, *op. cit.*

23. *16–18s in Scotland—An Action Plan*. SED. 1983. p. 60.

24. Kirk, Gordon. *The Core Curriculum*. Hodder and Stoughton. 1986. p. 69.

25. *Ibid.*, p. 101.

SELECT BIBLIOGRAPHY

Bone, T. R., *School Inspection in Scotland*. University of London Press. 1968.

Consultative Committee on the Curriculum. *The Social Subjects in Secondary Schools*. Curriculum Paper 15. 1976.

Consultative Committee on the Curriculum. *An Education for Life and Work*. 1983.

Consultative Committee on the Curriculum. *Primary Education in the Eighties*. 1983.

Consultative Committee on the Curriculum. *Education 10–14 in Scotland*. 1986.

Consultative Committee on the Curriculum. *Curriculum Design for the Secondary Stages*. 1987.

Gatherer, W. A. and Wallace, B., ed. *Educating for Tomorrow: A Lothian Perspective*. Holmes McDougall. 1984.

Humes, W. M., *The Leadership Class in Scottish Education*. John Donald. 1986.

Kirk, Gordon. *The Core Curriculum*. Hodder and Stoughton. 1986.

Kirk, Gordon. *Teacher Education and Professional Development*. Scottish Academic Press. 1988.

MacBeath, J., *Personal and Social Education*. Scottish Academic Press. 1988.

McPherson, A. and Raab, C. D., *Governing Education*. Edinburgh University Press. 1988.

Nisbet, J. and Kirk, Gordon. *Scottish Education Looks Ahead*. Chambers. 1969.

Richmond, W. Kenneth, *The School Curriculum*. Methuen. 1971.

Scottish Education Department. *Primary Education: A Report of the Advisory Council on Education in Scotland.* HMSO. 1946.

Scottish Education Department. *Secondary Education: A Report of the Advisory Council on Education in Scotland.* HMSO. 1947.

Scottish Education Department. *Primary Education in Scotland.* HMSO. 1965.

Scottish Education Department. *The Structure of the Curriculum in the Third and Fourth Years of the Scottish Secondary School.* HMSO. 1977.

Scottish Education Department. *Learning and Teaching in P4 and P7.* HMSO. 1981.

Scottish Education Department. *16–18s in Scotland: An Action Plan.* 1983.

Scottish Education Department. *Learning and Teaching in Scottish Secondary Schools: School Management.* HMSO. 1984.

Scottish Education Department. *Learning and Teaching in the First Two Years of the Scottish Secondary School.* HMSO. 1986.

Strathclyde Regional Council. *Managing Progress.* 1988.

Weir, A. Douglas, *Education and Vocation 14–18.* Scottish Academic Press. 1988.

INDEX